Guardians
— of the —
Salmon

PIONEERING CONSERVATION ON WESTCOUNTRY RIVERS

Gordon H. Bielby

First published in Great Britain in 2001

Copyright © 2001 Gordon Bielby
Copyright © 2001 illustrations Angela Brown

All rights reserved. No part of this publication may be reproduced, stored in a retrieval system, or transmitted in any form or by any means without the prior permission of the copyright holder.

British Library Cataloguing-in-Publication Data
A CIP record for this title is available from the British Library

ISBN 1 84114 139 9

HALSGROVE

Halsgrove House
Lower Moor Way
Tiverton, Devon EX16 6SS
Tel: 01884 243242
Fax: 01884 243325
email www.halsgrove.com

Printed and bound in Great Britain by Bookcraft Ltd, Midsummer Norton

CONTENTS

Introduction   5

Author's Notes   7

Acknowledgements   9

1. The Silver Swallow   11

2. Predators Must Die   29

3. Questions of Breeding   41

4. Plagues and Problems   61

5. Trouble at Mills   79

6. Bailiff Force   93

7. Portions of Poached Salmon   119

References   *144*

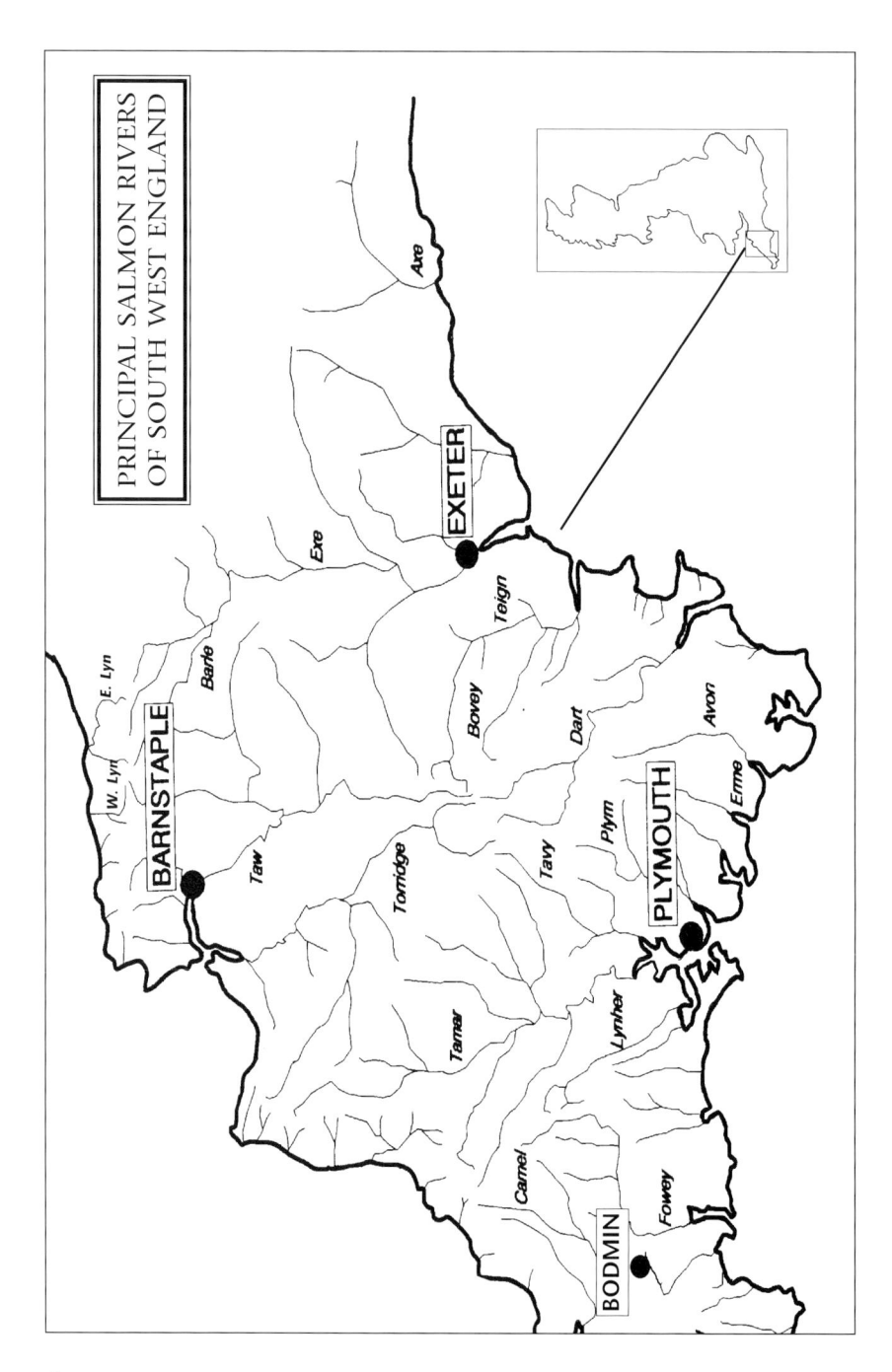

Guardians of the Salmon

Principal Salmon Rivers of South West England

INTRODUCTION

I do not claim to be a salmon expert and this is decidedly not a technical book.

Fascinating fish though it is, my interest has long been more in the people associated with the salmon than in, say, the finer points of its biology. Combine that approach with a preference for the 'old days', mix in my inclination to see the funny side of things, add a pinch or two of autobiography and you have the recipe for this book.

Guardians of the Salmon is a nostalgic look at efforts in bygone days to conserve the salmon. It is mainly – but not exclusively – about the life and times of the members who served on, and the bailiffs, fisheries officers and Clerks who worked for, the various bodies formed down the years for that purpose. It recalls their dealings with folk who in their different ways were involved in the salmon world, including: magistrates, millers, trappers, policemen, polluters, poachers, priests, reporters, solicitors, engineers, netsmen, fishery owners, anglers and inevitably some 'men from the Ministry'.

This is not a 'fishing book' in the sense of how, where and when to go angling for salmon (for I know nothing of such things) but a work that has more to do with subjects such as wildlife conservation, heritage, countryside, local history and the environment.

The anecdotes have a sound, factual basis, but since some were at least second-hand when they reached me (and one or two remarkably fresh considering their age) there may have been some distortion of the original happenings for which I apologise in advance. I am also guilty of embellishing a few to which, in mitigation, I plead artistic licence.

Guardians of the Salmon is meant to be a good read, whether you care about salmon or not.

I hope you will enjoy it!

GHB
Kenn
October, 2001

DEDICATION

For my wife Joice and our daughters Susan, Julie and Kathryn who waited long enough for 'Dad's book' to come out but never doubted that one day it would.

AUTHOR'S NOTES

1. This book draws most of its material from the period between 1860 and 1974, those being the days when the various Boards were the public guardians of the salmon. A few earlier and later events and references are included where they add colour to the narrative.

2. Although most of the anecdotes could be told of salmon rivers anywhere, they specifically relate to those of Cornwall and Devon in the south west of England, the catchments of which (not respecting local authority boundaries) also nudge into adjoining Somerset and Dorset.

3. Between 1860-1974, there was a succession of bodies with different constitutions, duties, powers and so on and all dabbling in salmon management. The process began with boards of conservators and fishery boards operating in nine main catchment areas designated as fishery districts: geographically these were the Taw and Torridge, Camel, Fowey, Tamar and Plym, Avon, Dart, Teign, Exe and Axe. To keep it simple, they are simply referred to in the text as, for example, the 'Fowey Board' or the 'Dart Board' [sic]. In 1950 three of these Boards (Camel, Fowey and Tamar and Plym) merged to become the Cornwall River Board while the others became the Devon River Board. These two bodies and their successors, the two river authorities, are just referred to respectively as the 'Cornwall Board' and the 'Devon Board' whatever the date of the reference.

4. River authorities themselves went out of favour in 1974, when they were absorbed within a new South West Water Authority, a reorganisation that for the author marked the end of the 'old days' that inspired this book.

5. Inevitably there was always a power in London controlling the Boards and just referred to here as the 'Ministry', whether or not at the time it was actually the Home Office, the Board of Trade, the Board of Agriculture and Fisheries, the Ministry of Agriculture Fisheries and Food or whatever.

6. Sums of money pre-decimalisation (1971) are in the old units: pounds, shillings and pence. (There were twelve old pennies in a shilling and twenty shillings in a pound. A guinea was twenty-one shillings, a crown five shillings and a sovereign was a gold coin worth nominally £1. One shilling was equivalent to five new pence.).

7. Mention of the Avon always means the beautiful Devon Avon.

8. Since river names are mentioned so often, to avoid possibly irritating repetition, the word 'River' and its abbreviation 'R.' have been omitted from river names throughout.

9. The detailed history of salmon fisheries administration is a dry subject, unsuitable for this book. Anyone interested is advised to go first to Warwick Ayton's informative and concise *Salmon Fisheries in England and Wales*, published in 1998, in the Atlantic Salmon Trust's 'Blue Book' series (available from AST, Moulin, Pitlochry, Perthshire, PH16 5JQ).

10. The 1860 Royal Commission is referred to throughout as the 'Salmon Commission'.

11. Chapter 6 (Bailiff Force) includes the aftermath in Tiverton of the murder in 1887 of Mr Archibald Reed, a bailiff of the local fishing association. I was conscious that – even after all that time – to include it might cause distress to the descendants of those who were involved and I have no wish for that to happen. I therefore wrote to the *Mid Devon Gazette* appealing for any such person to be in touch and they published my letter. Nine months on, I have still not heard from anyone in that category although others have kindly written with information.

12. Throughout this book, 'poaching' just means illegal fishing.

13. The office of 'Clerk' mentioned throughout was not the lowly position it sounds but a Board's chief executive officer and in the early years its only employee, apart from bailiffs. It was convenient for the post to be filled by a local firm of solicitors on a part time basis.

ACKNOWLEDGEMENTS

Annual reports, minutes and letter-books of the Boards have been consulted. Old newspapers have been studied in libraries at Exeter, Plymouth, Tiverton and Barnstaple. Museums were visited at Exeter, Tiverton, Barnstaple, Appledore, Topsham. Teignmouth and Totnes. At all of these locations, people were unfailingly helpful.

Invaluable was the text, copied to me by my friend Mr Dennis Mitchell CBE, of a lecture on the salmon and sea trout of the Teign, delivered in 1889 to the Torquay Natural History Society, by John Webster, then Hon. Sec. of the Lower Teign Fishery Association.

Another priceless source was the report of a Royal Commission on the state of the salmon fisheries. This was published in 1861 along with the verbatim minutes of evidence taken at their hearings and kindly sent to me by Dr David Solomon. To assist future researchers, a copy of these papers has been given to the Westcountry Studies Library in Exeter.

Colleagues at the former National Rivers Authority kindly contributed anecdotes, jogged my memory, did bits of research and offered much-needed encouragement. I am indebted to them all and am sure they will understand why I refrain from mentioning particular individuals.

Many other people helped in different ways and I thank them all including: George Garlick ; Amber Patrick; Mrs Pat Slade; G B Wyatt, FRCP; Dr J H Porter; Michael Nix; Alan Voce; Robert Lush; L J Davey; Derek Heard; Ian Scofield; Barbara Entwhistle; Bob Andrew; David Clement; Trevor Finbow; Mrs Patricia Mead; The Earl of Devon; Peter Hutchinson; David Chapman; N S Nathan, Ted Potter and Will Hellon.

Tribute is due also to a report by Mr J B S Notley, a copy of which was kindly sent to me by Mr Jim Coombes of the Avon Fishing

Association. It is an account of the state of the Devon Avon by a man who fished it for eighty years from 1899 when he was six.

Thanks also to the *Western Morning News* for allowing use of the photograph of Endsleigh Hatchery, to the Topsham Museum Society for that of the giant salmon and to Mrs Shelby Edworthy for that of her father, Mr Bill Newman. Martin Sowman and Angela Doughty, of Exeter Cathedral, could not have been more helpful than they were in finding, photographing and permitting me to use the picture of the deed of 1228.

I am especially grateful to my gifted friend, Angela Brown, for enriching the book with her drawings and contributing common sense and a few chuckles to its production.

Despite enquiries, including press coverage, I have been unable to find out who if anyone now owns the picture of the big catch on the Teign Estuary in 1922.

1
The Silver Swallow

Many years ago, I was asked by a reporter to say why, that year, there were more salmon than usual in the rivers of South Devon – a very rare circumstance indeed. Doubtless at his editor's behest, he wrote, as I recall, an excited piece about the good times ahead for local salmon fishermen. In the article he referred to the salmon as the 'Silver Swallow of the Seas' and said there was great joy at its returning. That apt description has always seemed to me to capture nicely the spirit of the salmon and so, with thanks to that unknown reporter, I have used it to head this opening chapter.

I should make it clear at the outset that the salmon we are dealing with are not the canned varieties (sold as Pink Salmon or Red Salmon) that, where I come from, used to be served as a treat for Sunday tea. Nor are we talking about those you may have seen on TV being caught and eaten by grizzly bears in Alaska. Those are all Pacific Salmon of which there are several species. This book is concerned only with the one species of Atlantic Salmon, *Salmo salar*, a fish that in the normal run of things would not be seen dead in a tin.

Fresh salmon enter the rivers from the sea throughout the year, nearly all on their 'maiden' spawning migration. As they mature they stop feeding and gradually lose their bright silver appearance, becoming darker and more coloured. The males develop a distinctive, hooked lower jaw (or 'kype') which looks fearsome but appears to be more for display than actual fighting. Although individual fish may return at any time, there are pronounced seasonal peaks or 'runs' when shoals of like fish come in together and rivers are spoken of as having runs of 'spring fish' or 'summer fish' and so on. It is believed that runs of the former have drastically declined in recent years as a result of the ills besetting the salmon.

When water conditions such as temperature and flow are right, salmon make their way upstream in search of spawning gravels. On that journey they may be seen trying to swim up or leap over the many weirs that still obstruct most rivers. As a wildlife spectacle this may not rank with a million wildebeest crossing the Serengeti, but it can be thrilling in a modest, British way and if you have not seen it then you should try to do so. Wherever you decide to watch and wait, first ask around (try the nearest pub) to make sure salmon can sometimes be seen there. A good time is when it rains hard after a dry spell. Be patient: give it at least half an hour, not just a passing glance... and watch out for bears!

Spawning normally takes place in November and December though I have seen it in March and heard of it as late as April. The female (or 'hen') does most of the work, digging a series of nests (or 'redds') in the river gravel. The male (or 'cock') remains nearby, awaiting his moment. When it arrives, the yolky eggs, like orange peas, are released to be fertilised by a cloud of sperm (or 'milt') discharged by the male. They settle safely between the stones where they are covered with gravel by the female. Although most of the adults die after spawning, a few (mainly female) 'kelts' (or 'back fish' in former times) make it back to the sea where they resume feeding and start to regain condition. The developing eggs remain in the gravel until the following spring when they hatch into delicate 'alevins' – tiny fish, each with its own food supply in a yolk sack attached to its belly. In 1861 Charles Dickens, in his weekly journal *All the Year Round*, explained:

> *Master and Miss fish have no kind nurse to give them their proper soft food but Nature, the kindest of nurses, has packed their food up for them in a pretty little bag which she has fastened on to... their bodies.*

Later, about an inch long and with yolk sacks absorbed, 'fry' emerge from the protection of the gravel and begin to feed on the natural food of the stream. They grow steadily, usually for two years, but sometimes one or three and become 'parr' (or 'heppers' in bygone days) with distinctive, thumb-print markings on their flanks. At this stage a casual observer may mistake them for young brown trout but the key distinguishing features of colouration, shape of fins, size of mouth, markings and so on, are easy enough to learn.

Not bothering to do so has always annoyed the bailiffs, so much so that in 1883 one even had a confiscated salmon parr preserved in a jar of spirit and displayed in a Tavistock shop window for all to look and learn.

An interesting aspect of salmon biology is that some male parr may become sexually mature and join in the act of spawning with adult females – Mother Nature's 'toy boys' so to speak. This precocious sexual activity is believed to weaken them, stunting their growth and lowering their resistance to disease. Even so, it is handy insurance against there being a dearth of ripe cock fish.

Each spring, still only a few inches long, those parr ready to do so turn into silver 'smolts' (or 'gravelling' in bygone days) and migrate down the rivers to the sea, their destination no longer a complete mystery. Thanks to tagging we now know many of them travel the two thousand miles and more to feed and fatten on the capelin, herring, sand-eels and other goodies in the rich waters off the west coast of Greenland. The records are fascinating. An example of the outward journey was a hatchery smolt, released in the Exe in March 1968, being taken off Godthåb (Greenland's capital, now called Nuuk) in September 1969. An example of the return leg occurred in October 1971 when scientists aboard a Danish research vessel, drift-netting off west Greenland, caught, tagged and released a salmon that eight months later was taken by an angler on the Tavy. Many similar journeys are on record.

The full story of how they find their way over such vast distances remains one of Mother Nature's secrets, but the stars, earth's magnetic field and ocean currents are all likely to be involved. So is some form of chemical memory that enables a homing salmon to detect and recognise its own river. Back in 1889 John Webster offered an explanation in his lecture to the Torquay Natural History Society:

> *The salmon must have his sea marks too, the ocean bed is not all bare. There are currents instead of rivers, great shallows that once were mountain tops, huge wrecks where navies fought and sunk. He can have no difficulty finding the pathway to his home amidst the stillness of the deep.*

In the early 1960s, with colleagues, I began studying the area's salmon to discover what I could about their biology as a basis for better management. We examined thousands of scales from salmon caught by netsmen and anglers who collected them for me as part of special investigations. We had particularly helpful netsmen on the Dart and on summer evenings, when the tides were right for netting, we would go down to its estuary at Stoke Gabriel to help with the good work. This was an undemanding task, further eased by the need to base our operations in the village pub, the public bar of which was akin to a fishing 'ops room', an ideal place to be when the men came trickling up from the river for a beer and a moan about the fishing. They were only too pleased to let us weigh their catch and take a few scales while they offered advice and sank pints.

Scale samples were taken by scraping a knife along the shoulder of a fish and then wiping scales and slime into a small envelope – a messy business, to be done without damaging the fish and reducing its value. It was often weeks before the samples were examined, by when they had dried rock-hard. Each little clump had to be loosened so the scales could be cleaned and a few selected under a microscope for mounting on glass slides. This was achieved by soaking them overnight in a solution of warm water and Tide washing powder – a technical advance we were proud of.

To read scales we preferred to project their enlarged images onto a screen, thus making it easier for us to discuss difficult cases. We soon found the reading of large collections to be more a recognition of patterns than fine scrutiny of the material. There is a familiar look to the scales of an age class when you have seen a few hundred of them. It was useful also to be able to refer to the scale collections of Mr Ian Cameron, a North Devon veterinary surgeon who had examined hundreds of salmon for the Devon Board.

When considering the findings of these studies we had to remind ourselves we were only looking at scales from salmon caught 'in season' (roughly spring and summer) and also that our sampling-rate was very uneven, if for no other reason than boredom as the season wore on. A token payment of a few pennies a packet to official collectors was hardly enough for them to turn professional and sample more evenly. For all that, we felt justified in reaching a few broad, general conclusions about the salmon that made up the catch in the early 1960s.

Most smolts were two years old when they went to sea though some went after one year and others after three. Some of the incoming fish (called 'grilse') had spent one winter at sea while others were away for up to four sea-winters. An absence of one or two sea-winters was the norm, three was less common and four rare. Nearly all fish died after spawning so very few scales had even one mark recording a previous return to the river.

About that time we also began to survey the salmon rivers to find out how many fry and parr there were and get some idea of their distribution. This was done by means of a then new technique of electric-fishing in which a current from a generator was passed into the water via electrode poles held by a survey crew. Fish in the electric field swam helplessly towards the electrodes. They were then removed with a net and held in what we called a 'live car' (a metal frame, covered in fine-mesh netting and placed in the flow of the stream) before being identified, counted, measured and returned to the water. Spaced miles apart on the chosen river, sections about a hundred yards long would be isolated with stop nets and as many fish as possible removed during sweeps with the electrodes. The catch was handled in troughs kept topped-up with stream water and data were called-out to a recorder trying hard to keep a notebook dry.

Such surveys yielded a great deal of information about young salmon in the river systems and were worthwhile for that alone. They were however dangerous – electricity and water being a potentially lethal combination. Luckily only a few people felt a 'tingle' and nobody was seriously hurt. The nearest thing to a worrying incident came when the gear was being used to try and rescue a score or so of adult salmon stranded in a deep pool below turbines at a water works. A flat-bottomed boat was deployed with two men aboard: one using the electrode pole and the other standing-by with a dip-net. Not designed for use in deep water, the electrode was not attracting these lethargic fish despite the operator trying for depth by throwing it spear-like at them. Suddenly the netsman lost his footing, went overboard and disappeared. As he came gasping to the surface, his mate instinctively proffered the live pole for him to grab. Fortunately, it was beyond his reach.

These surveys were later realised to have demonstrated successful salmon spawning on a scale that would soon be a thing of the past. At site after site in the upper reaches, the first touch of the electric current would stun a multitude of beautiful silvery fry. Some were salmon, some were trout but in such numbers they had to be recorded as 'too numerous to count', let alone identify.

South West salmon rarely weigh more than 20lb. Most are much lighter but heavier fish do occur and a few beauties are on record. In 1899, according to Augustus Grimble's *The Salmon Rivers of England and Wales*, a 40lb kelt was landed from the Exe at Salmon Pool, to that date the largest fish ever seen on the river. On a date noted only as 'pre-1914', a kelt of 41lb was poached from the Avon. The poacher may also have been caught for weighing was done at the home of the Chairman of the Avon Board. A fish of 42lb fell to a Taw and Torridge netsman in 1942 and the Superintendent of that Board in 1948 said there were fish up to 50lb on the spawning beds but that was probably just another way of saying they were really big. The heaviest I have seen weighed $38^{1}/2$lb and had been caught in the Exe nets at Topsham. It had spent two years in the river, then four at sea before returning.

A giant salmon of $61^{1}/4$lb was caught by a Mr Dick Voysey of Topsham on 18 March 1924 at Counterfeit Sands, Starcross, on the Exe Estuary. This magnificent specimen had also spent two years in the river, but then a freakish five at sea before its first and fatal return. It was reported that a Captain Crisford, of Macfisheries Ltd, bought it and gave it to the Exe Board who had it mounted and presented it to Exeter Museum. Naturally it has become a famous fish, with its image and those of its proud captors illustrating many a local book and even featuring on a large wall-painting in the town. At the time of writing (2001) it is in Topsham Museum, revered as the authenticated monster – but of course there were bigger ones that got away.

Two thousand years ago, the rivers teemed with salmon and our forbears caught them with simple spears, much as poachers do today. Salmon came and went with the seasons, more in some years than others – good times and bad according to natural laws. Fresh in from the sea, their rich, oily flesh must have been a regular and welcome feast. Though skilled with a spear, man took only enough for his needs and did the rest no harm – a way of fishing that could have lasted indefinitely. Professor W. G. Hoskins, in his *Two Thousand Years in Exeter*, described the Exe as 'teeming with salmon', the word 'Exe' itself, he said, coming from an old British word meaning 'a river abounding in fish'.

Early travellers in the region mentioned salmon in their journals. In 1669 an observer from Tuscany noted that the rivers around Plymouth produced a 'great quantity' of salmon and that renowned travelling lady Celia Fiennes, passing through Exeter, saw them being speared while leaping at weirs on the Exe. Crossing the Tamar in 1724, Daniel Defoe thought it held 'vast numbers' of good fat salmon. There is a well-known story that later, while leaning over a Totnes bridge, he saw a trap in which the Dart's ebbing tide had stranded sixty 'small salmon' in a foot or so of water. His companion, the landlord of an inn by the bridge, fixed a net at one end of the trap and put his trained dog in at the other to drive the fish into it. Mr Defoe and his friends dined on six that night for a shilling, marvelling at the 'cheapness and plenty' of such splendid food. Things were much the same fifty years later when William Marshall, a keen student of rural affairs, toured the area noting salmon in 'considerable plenty' at Bideford Market and in 'great abundance' in the rivers of the Plymouth district.

Some of these tales were perhaps a shade exaggerated. When William Hals wrote of 'infinite numbers' of salmon being taken from the Camel in the seventeenth and eighteenth centuries, it maybe just seemed a lot at the time. Yet there must have been plenty of salmon about to excite so many witnesses. In his Torquay lecture, John Webster warned against taking the word of old men who look back through 'rose-coloured spectacles' and might be expected to claim that the Teign, or any other river for that matter, was once teeming with fish. Even so, considering these observations and allowing for a little exaggeration, it seems certain that salmon were formerly abundant throughout the area and had been so from when the species first evolved.

No tales of salmon galore would be complete however without mention of the apprentices who are said to have had clauses in their contracts that they were not to be fed salmon more than two or three times a week. This story persists wherever there are salmon rivers but nobody has yet been able to produce documentation to prove it. Many have claimed sight of such papers. George Pulman, in his *Book of the Axe*, said he had actually seen indentures for apprentices to a fellmonger and to a baker. Unfortunately both had been destroyed after the deaths of those concerned, but he felt sure their relatives would corroborate his statement. However, a few years later, the Chairman of the Axe Board was still appealing in the press for any such papers to be produced for inspection.

The intriguing question is: why would such clauses have been thought necessary? Maybe the fish were foul. Take the case of boys working for farmers living near the Tavy. Around Christmas time, these gentlemen salted down, in granite troughs and red earthenware crocks (or 'salters'), as many salmon as they could catch. Their boys were on the typical contract specifying they not be fed salmon more than three days a week. Even if the fish had been fresh when caught (highly unlikely) preserved in salt they must soon have become pretty rank and it is easy to imagine these lads thinking salmon three times a week was thrice too often. So, maybe that was it – the fish were just virtually inedible.

Why the apprentices had these contracts (if they did have them) is a mystery that has long puzzled the salmon world and neither before nor since have I seen the explanation that came from a *History of Cornwall*, by a Reverend R. Polwhele, published in 1806. Speculating as to why leprosy had disappeared from the county, he reasoned it must surely have been caused by something that, like the awful disease itself, had gone away, concluding:

> *The prevailing notion is that leprosy was generated by the eating of salmon too frequently and at unseasonable times. That our forefathers thought so is evident from covenants that I have seen... stipulating that no apprentices or servants shall be obliged to dine on salmon more than once or twice a week. And we are told that in consequence of a due abstinence from salmon, lazar houses became no longer necessary.*

Lazar houses were leper hospitals. Far from being pampered, the apprentices were being protected from the horrors of leprosy by limiting their intake of salmon. It must have been a major health scare and it is a wonder anyone ever ate salmon again. To this day, fishmongers must hope no Minister ever decides to deny that there was once thought to be a connection between eating salmon and catching leprosy. Ironically, eating salmon is now thought to be a good thing because they are a rich source of certain oils that reduce the risk of heart disease and other conditions of unhealthy, modern lifestyles.

By the 1800s, how often salmon was fed to apprentices became an academic question for the fish were no longer there for the serving. Running true to form, man had so abused this great natural resource that in 1860 a Royal Commission was appointed to:

> *enquire into the Salmon Fisheries of England and Wales, with the view of increasing the supply of a valuable article of food for the benefit of the public.*

The Chairman was Sir William Jardine and with fellow Commissioners William Ffennell and George Rickards, he held public hearings around the South West at which witness after witness gave evidence about the awful state of the rivers and the plight of their salmon. The Town Clerk of Exeter, for instance, said that fisheries on the Exe, let for £50 back in 1601, had not been let for years. Moreover, only a small proportion of salmon sold in the city came from its own river – the same Exe that formerly had been 'teeming' with them. The Commissioners listened, questioned, deliberated, then reported several causes: fish passage was obstructed, there was too much trapping, there were no proper close seasons, there was confusion about the law, illegal fishing was rife and many rivers badly polluted. Apart from that, everything was fine.

The publication of their report in 1861 was a turning point in the fight to save the salmon but long before that lonely voices were clamouring for action. In 1824, J. Cornish in his book *A View of the Present State of the Salmon and Channel Fisheries*, described the sorry state of affairs and offered some original remedies. He said the Dart was blocked by traps and swept with nets but nobody cared. He proposed a new law with what he thought were proper penalties. For possessing salmon spawn or the young fish on their way to sea, he wanted a £20 fine for a first offence, £50 for a second and whipping or a year's hard labour for a third. Being caught on a river bank at night with a lantern or 'other fire' deserved 'transportation beyond the seas' for seven years. We may recoil from such penalties but I have met fishermen who would think them far too soft.

Shocked and possibly shamed by the Salmon Commission's grim verdict, yet encouraged by Parliament's rapid response, people at last began to act, demonstrating a recognition that something had to be done. So, one winter's day in 1862, there was a large gathering in Exeter to form a Board of Conservators for the Exe. As was the custom, proceedings were reported verbatim in the press. Some prominent local gentlemen attended, their speeches reflecting a broad cross-section of contemporary concerns.

Sir Stafford Northcote opening the meeting, explained that an Act had been passed in 1861 directing magistrates to appoint conservators whose 'special business' it would be to see that the provisions of the Act were put into effect. Unfortunately, both Exeter City and Devon County Benches had jumped the gun and already done so and therefore more gentlemen had been put forward than were needed. With goodwill that was soon resolved and the speeches began.

The Earl of Devon welcomed a new weekend close period for mills and traps which would allow salmon free passage on two days a week at least. Because of their quite extraordinary breeding powers, this would soon see more food available for the people and it was therefore in the public interest to remove obstacles to their migration. He reminded those present that Devon was ideal for sport fishing but that was a small matter compared with increasing food for the people. He then moved a resolution that if the provisions of the new legislation were followed, the Exe would return to its former position as one of the best salmon rivers in the land. This was carried unanimously.

Mr Ralph Sanders advocated using breeding ponds that could be built 'at trifling expense' to rear thousands of salmon fry. He informed the meeting that a gentleman from Clitheroe was in the area on his way to start a hatchery on the Tamar and perhaps his advice could be sought for the Exe. In two or three years, said Sanders, they would have a river well stocked with fish again – artificial breeding he claimed, to cries of 'hear! hear!', was easy and the only way to satisfy public food supply needs. He was not, he said, speaking as a sportsman. The Earl of Devon was also worried that the sewage from Exeter's forty thousand people found its way to the river and formed a serious obstacle to salmon. To shouts of encouragement, he said something should perhaps be done about it. One speaker suggested it be used to fertilise the marshes downstream of the city.

Sir Lawrence Palk, one of two MPs present, proposed a committee be formed, supported by an honorary trio of secretary, treasurer and solicitor and that was duly done. For all the worthy talk of feeding the public, a familiar underlying theme could be detected when one of these newly-appointed officers was commended as being not only a first-rate fisherman but a good fox hunter and sportsman as well.

Mr Samuel Kekewich, the other MP, appealed to millers and manufacturers for their 'cordial assistance' in carrying out the Act, for without their support it would not matter how many gentlemen they appointed that day to the Board. Millers were sharply criticised for running their mills as fish traps. One named Snow, who was at the meeting, defended his trade claiming that for years people had

21

jumped unreasonably to the conclusion that men on river banks wearing white hats were millers out poaching.

Lord Courtenay complained that unclean salmon could still be exported to France, so the incentive to poaching remained – 'the snake had been scotched, not killed'. Another speaker said that even if landowners co-operated, everyone knew how easy it was for a labourer to spear a fish with his pitchfork. As ever, the poor had to be blamed for something.

The Mayor pointed out they still had much to do, dinner would be on the table at five and it was four already. They quickly passed the necessary resolutions, appointed Sir Stafford as their Chairman and adjourned to the nearby Half Moon Hotel for what must have been a riotous dinner, also fully reported in the press.

The Chairman began the formalities with the Loyal Toast and then proposed the health of the Bishop and Clergy of the Diocese. He was sorry the Dean of Exeter could not be with them but he was like a salmon, 'a fish of passage' who had come amongst them for a while and then 'gone to See' – a rather ambitious pun in the circumstances. They then toasted the magistrates, the Lord Lieutenant, the House of Lords, the House of Commons, the Mayor, their own fishing club and the MPs present. Responding, Sir Lawrence said he had done little, having never known the House so eager to pass a Bill, attributing this to associations that were 'friends of the unprotected females' – a reference greeted with laughter for reasons hard to discern. The Chairman then rose through the smoke and din claiming it unfair that MPs had to make speeches during their close season. At this point the reporter gave up, closing his piece with a feeble 'further toasts and speeches followed'. It had been a splendid event: they had formed a Board, elected its Chairman, exposed some issues, resolved what needed to be done and enjoyed a dinner to mark the occasion.

I take the generous view that the efforts of such Boards and their later versions, at least slowed the rate of decline so that salmon appeared to be flourishing when I arrived on the scene a century after the Salmon Commission had reported. Despite constant grumbles that things were not what they used to be, to me the resource seemed in good shape. It was a while before I realised there had been a great decline... and it was still under way.

I was lucky enough to work for both the Devon Board (1960–66) and the Cornwall Board (1967–74) in their final decades and am often asked what it was like in those days. I was too junior to know much of the Devon Board beyond my job, but I recall its daunting Fisheries and Pollution Committee that I attended in a supporting role. Their salmon work was the routine administration of licences, catch returns, offence reports and so on blended with some of the more interesting things as described in this book. The Devon Board was then still only semi-detached from Devon County Council from which parts of it had sprung and with which for years it had shared some senior officers and facilities.

The Cornwall Board was more typical of its kind at that time – effective within the limits of its powers and finances. It had twenty-odd members, representing various interests and appointed by both Ministers and local councils. All were men. All served for free. Business was done through committees and confirmed at regular meetings of the Board. These were orchestrated by the Chairman who would go smartly through the agenda announcing who would propose and who would second each item for decision. Unanimous agreement was the norm and a committee chairman could count himself honoured if he got to present his own minutes. Any deals needed to ensure things went smoothly were done quietly behind closed doors, perhaps over a gin-and-tonic.

Drinks apart however, they neither offered nor themselves enjoyed corporate hospitality in pursuit of their objectives. They were thrifty guardians of the public purse as well as of the salmon. Some of them however were wonderfully out of touch. For instance, one old boy with a military background, unfamiliar with trades union matters, told me it was nonsense that the lady he called 'that nice little girl in reception' should belong to a union for local government 'officers'. If there *had* to be unions, he believed there ought to be separate ones for 'officers' and 'other ranks'. This was about the jobs people did – not the people themselves – all of whom he treated with great courtesy, regardless of rank.

The Cornwall Board had a custom unique in my experience – the 'Chairman's Conference'. The office operated a system requiring a carbon copy of all outgoing post to be circulated daily for the information of management colleagues. Once a week, the Chairman would lodge himself in his room with his Vice-Chairman and summon people to account for and be interrogated about their letter-book entries. Why had what been written to whom, was the game. In my early days there, fresh from Canada and still a bit brash, I had to appreciate that some people needed more *sensitive* treatment, there being issues that I was unaware of, and so on. It was a tight ship and so it had to be with the Vice-Chairman a retired senior officer of the Royal Indian Navy. When he became Chairman, conferences were more frequent but less formal and seldom passed the hour of six without a little spirit to help our discussions.

One thing hardly ever mentioned was fishing, because I did not fish and must digress for a moment to explain. From the outset, the Devon Board had made it pretty clear that I would be wise to decline politely the invitations to fish that would come my way. I was there for the *fish* not the fishing and it would be all too easy to owe favours, become aligned with the anglers, or appear to be so. It was not an order but a broad hint and I took it. I have always felt comfortable with that position but it has at times raised eyebrows and in Canada it was met with incredulity. But in my genes there was no yearning to fish, my only experience of it being a hand-line off the harbour wall in my home town of Scarborough and even that with little joy. Years later, the Clerk to the Cornwall Board tried to convert me. A taster was arranged at Anne Voss Bark's renowned Arundell Arms Hotel in Lifton where world-class tutors tried in vain to teach me to cast a line with my posh new trout rod. It was not their fault that when play was abandoned that day, it was never resumed.

Such diversions aside, I believe that as its end approached there had evolved by the 1970s a version of the Board system that was not 'broke' and did not need 'fixing', thereby making it certain to be changed. Although far from perfect, it could have been adjusted and adapted as necessary. As it was the last Boards were incomparably better than the Boards of earlier times which attracted the following comment in Fort and Brayshaw's 1961 classic work, *Fishery Management:*

...very little was done by those Boards beyond signing on two or three water bailiffs, handing them warrants, and telling them to keep an eye on the poachers...

Although there were still a few salmon traps operating, nearly all the legitimate fishing was by so-called commercial men in the estuaries and angling gentlemen – who claimed to fish for the love of it – in the rivers. A near-constant state of war prevailed between these blocs with each for ever accusing the other of taking too many fish, threatening livelihoods and sport respectively. Some of the Boards tried to educate the netsmen, believing their hostility stemmed from an ignorance of salmon biology. Come the back-end therefore, they would grit their teeth and guide bus-loads of them around the spawning areas to see the fish doing their stuff. To be fair, these gestures were well-meant and the more enlightened Board members tried hard to bring the net and rod interests closer together. A few netsmen became Ministry appointed Board members where they were well respected and influential. Others had to make do with being on area advisory committees, widely derided as 'talking shops'.

The ancient public right to fish for salmon in tidal waters had long been absent in practice because a licence was needed and these were no longer available on demand. By the last year of the Boards (1973), there were just over a hundred licences issued annually, many through a system of Net Limitation Orders, designed broadly to favour existing holders and genuine fishermen. Dealing with these valuable documents was taken so seriously that it was usually delegated to a special group of Board members whose unenviable duty it was to study written applications, interview applicants and decide who were the lucky ones, always with the prospect of legal challenge looming over them.

Licensees were declaring a combined annual catch of little more than ten thousand salmon. They were comprehensively regulated as to where, when and how they might lawfully fish but, despite the many regulations, they still applied for licences and complained that things were not what they used to be. Alas, that was all too true. Where salmon netting had once employed over a hundred men on the Exe alone, only a handful still relied upon it. Yet, hard work though it was, many still went netting because it was in their blood. Nevertheless, it did not take much imagination to see it before long as a heritage attraction with tame crews paid to go through the motions for the amusement of tourists.

It was already a far cry from the days when record catches were always on the cards as when eighty-nine salmon were caught in two hauls of a net at Shaldon on the Teign Estuary in 1922. It would have been more had not some escaped. The lucky netsmen were pictured posing proudly by this great pile of fish, each holding a specimen for a picture so remarkable that it was turned into a postcard for the resort.

Another famous catch occurred on the Exe Estuary in March 1937 when netsmen took ninety-seven salmon in one haul on the opening day of the season. From somewhere, I have acquired notes that purport to be of an interview a bailiff had with one of that crew over thirty years later. It makes interesting reading. They had sailed to the netting stations, sure there were salmon about. When they reached the spot, the crews already there had caught only a few and were packing up. Although there were only fifteen minutes to the turn of the tide and an end to fishing for that day, one of them was so certain there were salmon to be had that they shot the net once more. This time the heavy, old, cotton net nearly burst with the strain of the catch and the boat was loaded to the gunwales with salmon on their happy trip home. The haul went for just over a shilling a pound and as usual the proceeds were divided to give a share for each of the crew plus one for the boat and one for the net. The story-teller had bought a Harris Tweed suit with his share and said he would have been still wearing it had his shape not changed.

But those were very special days. Fishing was normally far less rewarding and vulnerable to many things beyond the control of netsmen. So, while a great Victorian event like the coming of the railways led to a tenfold increase in the price of salmon locally, it also made sellers dependent on trains to reach London's markets and in deep trouble if they did not run. During the General Strike of 1926, the Tamar and Plym netsmen had to halve their price to shift their fish. On the Exe, buyers at the salmon auctions were offering a mere sixpence a pound, so the fishermen told them – though perhaps not in these words – to catch the fish themselves if that was all they were worth.

There was 'a war on' for much of the time of this book and various predictable shortages, restrictions and so on are mentioned. However war also touched fishing in less expected ways. Camel salmon netsmen, for instance, during the Second World War, complained to their Board about the War Regulations for their estuary. For fairly obvious reasons, these declared that no boat was allowed to navigate at night or in 'thick weather', thereby severely restricting nocturnal drift-netting. Finding that the rules could not be relaxed, they settled for a refund of half their £2 licence duty, which may have been their goal anyway.

In 1941 an incident illustrated how the urgent cause of national survival could collide with routine business. A bailiff patrolling the Fowey came across a weir that the military had built to supply water to their camp at a place called Doublebois. It stretched right across the river and, war or no war, it would not do. The bailiff reported it to his Clerk. Months of officious correspondence and meetings on-site ensued with the Clerk demanding that the officer commanding the troops provide a fish-pass so salmon would not be denied access to wonderful spawning above the weir. This is not suggesting the Clerk should have acted any other way but noting with interest that such things still go on at such times.

In non-tidal waters, there was a wide range of fishery ownership including individuals, syndicates, hotels, clubs and even time-share. A few of the hotels had established national and even international reputations based on being able to offer salmon fishing to their guests. The Arundell Arms at Lifton, the Half Moon at Sheepwash, the Rising Sun at Umberleigh, the Black Horse at Torrington, the Fox and Hounds at Eggesford and the Carnarvon Arms at Dulverton were a few of the most popular at the time. Fishing associations with sizable memberships were more a feature of Cornwall than of Devon.

Anyone wanting to go fishing had also to buy a licence and these were still available on demand and payment of the duty. When the

Boards' era ended, a few hundred rod licensees were declaring an annual catch of well under five thousand salmon. How true these catches were was anyone's guess for there were liars in both net and rod camps declaring well below what they had actually caught. One shameless angler, faced with a reservoir proposal on his river, asked if he and his fishing friends could revise their declared catches for recent seasons to bring them nearer their true levels. They had wanted to keep the truth from the fishery's owner, for fear he would raise their rent, but the looming threat made it imperative to show how good the fishing really was. So much for catch statistics!

However, from the legions of rod fishermen have also come the most effective champions of salmon conservation and it would be wrong to put all that down to self-interest. Even so, those who go salmon fishing for fun have an apparent contradiction to explain. This was highlighted when a revered ex-military gentleman, renowned for his views on the sad state of salmon stocks, caught one so big and handsome that he featured with it in the newspapers. Proudly clutching his trophy, he was reported to be deeply concerned about the future of the species – to the uninitiated, a sentiment at odds with killing its finest specimens.

2
Predators Must Die

Man has long thought he could and should interfere with the natural order of things and do better than Mother Nature. He has never felt obliged to stand and watch predators take his salmon and any creature that could do so has been considered fair game.

Cormorants and shags, being partial to salmon, have long headed the hit-list. That they take smolts is undeniable. A colleague was once tagging wild smolts by fixing tiny metal discs to their backs with silver wire. It was a sunny day and he could see the tags glittering in a way he thought might attract predators. To put his mind at ease, he waited for a few days after releasing the smolts, then visited cormorant nests on the nearby coast. Against all the odds and after much smelly poking about, he was dismayed to find one of his tags glistening in the guano. He had shown that a shiny object attached to a smolt may attract a predator. If that be a cormorant and it eats the smolt, said object may pass through the bird to its droppings – a conversational gem down the pub perhaps, but hardly his Nobel Prize for Science.

The Boards were obsessed with cormorants and shags and did their utmost to exterminate them. In 1902 the Clerk to the Exe Board told his members that the steps they had taken to destroy cormorants (posting 'Wanted' notices and paying sixpence on every head produced to the Chairman) had met with approval in all quarters. Over 250 had been killed in just ten months. The following year this 'ridding of the river' continued and at least another 120 were destroyed. Many others were shot but not recovered for confirmation of the kill. They knew nothing of the diet of these birds apart from hearing that one shot in Cornwall had eaten 'six or so samlets'. Exe Estuary fishermen were unanimous that small fish were thriving as a result of the shooting. Stimulating the slaughter were bounty payments (by then a shilling a head) subscribed by 'certain gentlemen' who preferred to remain anonymous. The Dart Board were paying the same on heads delivered to specially-appointed agents, while the Tamar and Plym Board formed a Cormorant Committee to decide their 'head money' or 'capitation fee'.

Although hundreds were shot every year, the Exe Board were still complaining in 1935 that large numbers of them could be seen on their estuary. They blamed Devon County Council for making much of it a bird sanctuary. The Clerk to the Tamar and Plym Board meanwhile was alarmed to hear of a proposal to have cormorants and shags added to the list of protected birds. That would never do: everyone knew how numerous they already were and how they regularly hunted far inland. He had recently shot one thirty miles from the sea. Another, killed by a bailiff, had eaten eight salmon smolts, enough for the Board to fire off a strong protest against any further protection for these detested birds.

That year the Exe Board heard an interesting report. A cormorant shot on the Exe had been ringed in Scotland six months earlier. This and later work proved that however many were shot there would always be incoming migrants to replace them. The shooting continued.

Nor was duty neglected during the Second World War when in 1943 the Teign Board applied to the War Agricultural Council for cartridges to allow cormorants to be shot. They were sent only fifty – ammunition being needed on other fronts. In 1946, on the nearby Exe, payments were handed out on 360 heads proving there were still plenty of birds to shoot at when they had cartridges. A change of tactics was called for, so adjoining Boards planned a combined, sea-borne assault on cormorant, coastal breeding areas. Mercifully, bad weather kept this 'C-Day' invasion fleet in harbour long enough for second thoughts to prevail.

To the east, the Axe Board were very anti-shag. In 1927 they even staged a Cormorant Week of which, fortunately for the squeamish, no details are to hand. Four years later, they raised their bounty to five shillings and put a Mr Head [sic] in charge of culling. At a later meeting, they gave him a hearty vote-of-thanks and read out a letter, signed by grateful fishermen, congratulating them on fighting off the cormorant menace. Head had done his deadly job well.

The Cornwall Board ended their bounty scheme in 1959, though not for love of cormorants. They had been paying-out on birds shot anywhere in their area until they began to doubt the wisdom of doing so: was for instance a bird killed on the coast doing any damage to their interests? They decided probably not and stopped paying after regularly doing so on at least four hundred and sometimes over six hundred heads a year.

Soon afterwards the Devon Board, responding to mounting pressure from bird preservation interests, followed suit. After all, there was no actual evidence that cormorants or shags were harming salmon stocks or that shooting some of them would make any difference. They were also aware of heads being imported from up-country for their higher rewards, so these were ended and, officially at least, the birds could fly and fish in peace.

Ending the scheme brought the writer welcome relief from having to count and certify for payment the severed heads brought in by bounty hunters. Since their usual practice was to collect enough to make a trip worthwhile, they were often putrid when presented. Strangely enough, there was never much interest in auditing those bounty payments.

The Boards had however been acting in good faith, truly believing that if the 'black plague' could be shot from the skies there would be more salmon in their rivers. A reader once wrote to *Trout and Salmon* fishing magazine about this 'repulsive, reptilian bird' which he said ate three times its own weight of fish daily. Bemoaning the end of bounty schemes, he boasted of having shot hundreds of cormorants in his time. He and a friend had recently killed forty by lying in wait for them at dawn: they were a deadly menace that must be given no quarter. Lemon Gray in his classic *Torridge Fishery* had little time for them either when he wrote:

> *The only thing to be said in favour of the cormorants is that they make a most satisfying 'plonk' when a .22 bullet hits them.*

Though admired for their fishing skills, herons have long been another target. In 1906 the Exe Board put a bounty on them and thirty-five were destroyed in two years for a shilling apiece. The Dart Board tried a cheaper approach, asking heronry owners on the river to 'keep the birds down' to protect fish stocks. The owners refused, saying the birds were less numerous than in former years. Over on the Tamar, the Duke of Bedford's team of private bailiffs were shooting up to a dozen a year. They reckoned herons must be damaging their fishery because they had killed one with eighteen young salmon in its stomach.

During the Great 1914–18 War, the Dart Board put a bounty on herons and had their bailiffs shooting them on Dartmoor as and when they saw fit. This earned them a rebuke from the Duchy of Cornwall who were 'inclined to foster bird life' so could not sanction the carrying of guns by bailiffs. In 1923 bounty payments were made on only five birds from the lower reaches of the river. Thinking this a poor show, they doubled the reward to five shillings and unleashed a storm of protest from around the country. Letters poured in, the Clerk at one meeting reporting receipt of seventy-five. The Royal Society for the Protection of Birds and the Selbourne Society were outraged. Under pressure, the Board said they would not pay the bounty on birds shot in June, July or August, which they claimed was the breeding season. They were not inclined to accept evidence to the contrary. One protester had picked up bits of hatched eggs in a Dart heronry in March, proving early nesting. He even enclosed the shells with his letter but the Board would not budge. Their Clerk advised that there was actually a close season from March to October so no rewards could be paid then. Having saved money on herons, they defiantly tripled their bounty on shags shot in the upper Dart Estuary.

Other birds have suffered too. Gulls were regarded as serious predators on the Dart and their destruction encouraged. The Ministry set-down the official position on gulls in their annual report for 1907. While appealing for evidence of damage done to salmon fry by fish-eating birds, they listed the usual suspects: black-backed gull, tern, cormorant and shag, and made it clear that Boards would need such evidence if they were to try and have its legal protection removed from any bird. However, they reminded Boards that the black-backed gull 'usually considered to be the most destructive of salmon smolts' was not on the schedule of protected birds and therefore there was 'no restriction upon the killing of it' by authorised persons.

Mute swans attracted hostility for appearing to eat salmon eggs and the insect food of fry. Addressing the Salmon Commissioners, an Exeter solicitor said they were a main cause of the Exe salmon's decline. He had observed them working what he took to be spawning beds in and around the city and, although admitting to never having seen a swan's innards examined, he just knew they were doing great harm. Despite being a lawyer he was quite prepared to have them shot on – in a manner of speaking – nothing more than a gut feeling.

In 1934 a lady told the Taw and Torridge Board that the stomachs of some pochard duck she had shot had contained young salmon. They would have had a price on their beaks in no time but for it being learned that they had only come inland during a cold snap. By 1974 the advance guard of what later became an unwelcome wave of immigrants, reached the area when a few goosanders poked their beaks into its dangerous skies. The writer never saw this handsome, sawbill duck on local rivers but recalls sometimes finding serrated beaks among heads presented for cormorant bounty payments.

Writing in 1824 Cornish complained that otters were abundant and a menace. He knew a man who, while fishing for spawning salmon, accidentally speared an otter that was after the same fish. It was intolerable that an otter should get in the way like that. A bounty of five guineas a head would, he felt sure, eliminate them within six months and just in case anyone was in any doubt, he summarised his feelings:

> The animal is a wanton slaughterer that will kill twenty salmon without eating one. They commit their greatest mischief at spawning time, when they hunt the fish as a dog does a hare, flying at their prey with the velocity of an arrow, never missing either wounding or taking.

In April 1874 the *North Devon Journal* reported that salmon fishing would begin in a few days and every rod could expect sport. However, an extraordinary number of dead salmon had been seen on the river banks – 'never was known the like'. Otters were to blame for sure, so the writer urged the Taw and Torridge Board to have their bailiffs get after them with gin traps. He was sure one otter did more harm to the river than all the boys that fished with rod and line. Just as well, or they would have had the bailiffs setting boy traps. In 1884 an angler complained to the Tamar and Plym Board that on nine occasions he had found large salmon killed by otters. Something had to be done. About the same time, by way of contrast, John Webster was writing of an old man he knew who loved nothing better than to see 'Mr Otter' fishing by a mill on the Bovey, a tributary of the Teign.

Otters were once so common on the Dart that its predator-loathing Board seriously believed them a mortal threat to the fisheries. With reports coming in daily of otters taking fish all along the river, they asked Dartmoor Otter Hounds to 'attend to them', an early euphemism for killing as many as possible. However, experience had taught them that the hounds were not all that effective so just to be on the safe side they gave their bailiffs the curiously vague (but no doubt adequate) instruction to kill otters 'to a small extent'.

There is surprisingly little mention of otters in records for the Taw and Torridge, the waters that inspired Henry Williamson's *Tarka the Otter*. In 1940 the Taw and Torridge Board heard there were many otters in the river but they took no action, their minds that year perhaps more concerned with the critical state of the war with Nazi Germany.

Otter hunts were once reported in newspapers as sporting events. A typical example from the *Tiverton Gazette* in July 1887 began by setting the scene. The usual ten couples of hounds had been taken to the meet which began on the Exe at five in the morning. A dozen or so ladies were present – a 'tolerably numerous' attendance. It was overcast and threatening thunder, a light drizzle doing nothing to dampen the spirits of those assembled. The unleashed hounds soon picked up the scent of an otter bitch and her two cubs. Said the report:

After some very pretty swimming up and down stream, one of the cubs was killed, but in somewhat tame fashion, the bulk of the pack being some distance off at the moment. It weighed seven pounds and was preserved whole as a trophy of the chase.

The other cub was then hunted to exhaustion but – canny hunters that they were – they let the 'varmint' escape to provide sport another day. The hounds then found the bitch 'working merrily' in a pool under a bridge. Giving her no rest for the next half-hour, they forced her to take to land where she was neatly 'rolled over' as she was making for her plunge. She weighed about sixteen pounds. Her mask and pads were removed in a field before the remains were thrown to the pack. They later came across the dog otter but the hounds were too weary to catch it. All present were said to have enjoyed a 'capital morning's sport'. In Tiverton Museum there is a poignant reminder of such days – an otter pole used to disturb animals seeking refuge under river banks. It bears notches recording kills on bygone sporting mornings.

The 1901 books of the Duke of Bedford's Endsleigh hatchery recorded the buying of otter traps. His Grace's private bailiffs regularly used to find salmon killed by otters so they used to trap a few to keep their hand in and boost the tally of the hounds. Like most big country estates, that of the Duke of Bedford was no place to be a predator – except one with two legs, a salmon rod and (most important of all) the Duke's blessing.

In the 1950s, some mink escaped, or were released, from local fur farms. Finding freedom to their liking, they rapidly colonised the area and within a decade hundreds were being caught and destroyed. Tighter controls were introduced for mink ranching, but it was too late – the beasts had bolted. Wild birds, fish and small mammals seemed most at risk, but creatures closer to man, such as racing pigeons, guinea-pigs, poultry and goldfish were also taken. Trapping failed to contain them and by 1970 they were pretty well part of the fauna. At large they soon gained a reputation as ruthless killers with an insatiable blood-lust. 'Duck Life in Peril as Mink Killers Rampage' screamed one headline as Totnes feared for its mallard. Some said they were killing lambs and mink hysteria grew. One paper warned parents not to leave babies outside in their prams lest hungry mink came their way. Affected interests demanded more trapping but the escapees were breeding too fast for that to do any good.

During the great mink madness, bailiffs sometimes confronted situations requiring much tact and initiative. One is recorded in a bailiff's report that I have to hand. He had been phoned by his local fishing club with the news that a mink had been captured. A lady who lived by the river had seen one clambering into her dustbin. On an impulse, she had rushed out, slammed down the lid and trapped the intruder within. For the bailiff, the tricky question of disposal now arose – but what was he to do? He phoned his Head Bailiff who said it was a matter for Headquarters who predictably thought he was best placed to decide. In truth he was on his own and his options were limited. He knew the lady to be of 'tender disposition' towards animals and, killer or not, she would not want the mink to suffer. On arrival at the scene, he learned the bin was full of rubbish so, with the river in spate, just taking it down to the water to drown the animal was not a good idea. Neither was his plan to blast it with a twelve-bore because any violence was out. To his great relief, the RSPCA, who had also been summoned, arrived with chloroform pad and lethal injection. The lady was satisfied. Not a pound had been spent. No blood had been shed. He still had all his fingers. The star of the show had gone to be stuffed at Plymouth Museum. For the bailiff it was just another day at the sharp end.

There was a short-lived hope that the wild mink would be worth trapping for their fur. From the pelts of those that were trapped, entrepreneurs fashioned a few purses and made fur-covered buttons that had a tatty, novelty appeal but without colder winters a quality fur industry was never really on the cards. Instead, mink mania gradually died down, hunts were formed to chase them with hounds, hatcheries set mink traps and that, more or less, was that.

Seals in this area are no great threat to salmon stocks. Occasionally one may take a fancy to an estuary for a while as happened once on the Exe estuary at Topsham where Sammy the Seal (they are always called 'Sammy') amused the crowds with his fishing skills. Fishermen were less impressed and restaurateurs claimed he was playing havoc with their menus by eating or frightening off all the salmon. 'We are definitely feeling the pinch' said one 'and it's all down to Sammy'. A few months later another exhibitionist was washed up near Totnes on the Dart estuary. He had been shot between the eyes. 'Anger Over Killing of Sammy the Seal' went the headlines and fishermen were outraged at losing a local character.

An effort was once made by the Cornwall Sea Fisheries Committee (doubtless encouraged by salmon interests) to eradicate grey seals from their north coast. In 1934, 177 were shot by marksmen with .303 rifles and a further 70 or so were accounted for each year until 1951. A scheme was in place whereby a reward of three shillings was paid for each seal head and stomach delivered to the Marine Biological Association in Plymouth. Apart from verifying the kill, it is difficult to see what a study of decaying seal parts was going to tell them. An annual limit of £50 was put on this enterprise, most of it going on ammunition.

Porpoises were once thought of as salmon's worst enemies. Cornish believed they prevented the fish from going out to sea, keeping them instead feeding amongst the coastal rocks. He thought these 'ravenous animals' drove salmon up the rivers and was convinced some method must be devised for taking them as their oil would 'richly repay' fishermen. He pointed out they were easily drowned when ensnared in a net and since they produced but one young at a time, they would soon 'not be recruited'. Frank Buckland, an Inspector of Salmon Fisheries, heard complaints about them at Fowey in 1872. They were preying on salmon from September to December, when many fat fish ran the river. As many as a hundred had been encircled in a seine net. Buckland agreed they should be captured and their oil sold.

In 1925 fishermen complained to the Tamar and Plym Board that porpoises were killing too many salmon but the Board decided to leave it to them to do what they could by shooting. Following further complaints, the Duke of Bedford employed two men to patrol the estuary to shoot the animals which took the hint and fished there less frequently. A decade later the matter was back on the agenda with the Clerk reporting complaints by the net fishermen of damage being done by porpoises. He cited a shoal seen surrounding and attacking salmon near Mashford Wharf. Porpoises were costing the netsmen dear for as well as feeding on salmon they were taking bites out of many more, thus greatly reducing their value. No effective action can have been taken for they used to appear every year as soon as salmon entered the river.

Other areas appeared less bothered although in the 1920s the Dart Board did spend fifty shillings on a man to shoot porpoises. The Taw and Torridge Board were asked to pay towards the cost of rifles to kill porpoises alleged to be doing terrible damage to the salmon fishery. A sub-committee decided there was no satisfactory way of dealing with them, so they would do nothing – refreshing wisdom that would have irked the writer of a letter to a local paper who wrote:

> *The ever-increasing number of porpoises entering our estuaries is making great inroads into our salmon stock. Absolutely nothing is done to these brutes as they plunge upstream.*

Predatory fishes were always severely dealt with. The big so-called 'cannibal' trout, found throughout the area, have an inclination to eat their younger, smaller relatives that has kept them at odds with fishermen. In former times they were routinely removed by owners and bailiffs using baited night-lines. In 1909 one diligent owner earned a vote-of-thanks from the Dart Board for killing three hundred that season. Selection of bait for such operations was a serious affair. Thus in 1927 did the full Dart Board solemnly consider quotations offering one hundred bottles of extra-large gudgeon for just over £12 and sprats, 'packed in tins semi-dry', at a shilling a dozen. As bait experts do – and they would all have been bait experts – they deliberated long and hard before ordering twenty-five bottles of the gudgeon.

If life was hard for elderly trout, it was even tougher for eels. The Cornwall Board boasted that wherever and whenever eels are found they are destroyed. Many bailiffs had an irrational loathing for these interesting fish and would behead any encountered, believing that to be the only sure way of killing them. Eels come into the rivers as elvers a few inches long and the Boards used to operate traps to intercept them. These were wooden, straw-lined troughs, inclined into the river to face what looked like a black ribbon of elvers hugging the banks as they swam upstream. Water trickling down the trough enticed some of the run to swim up it and fall into holding tanks at the top. Year after year, millions were taken this way. At first they were destroyed, but in later years they were sold to dealers who were said to export them live to eel farms. While the Boards firmly believed they were right to kill as many eels as possible, others wondered if, with fewer eels about, otters might be inclined to eat more salmon – a concern not tested as elver runs became less reliable and the Boards lost interest.

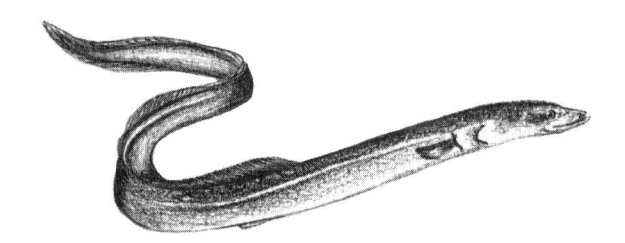

Guardians of the Salmon

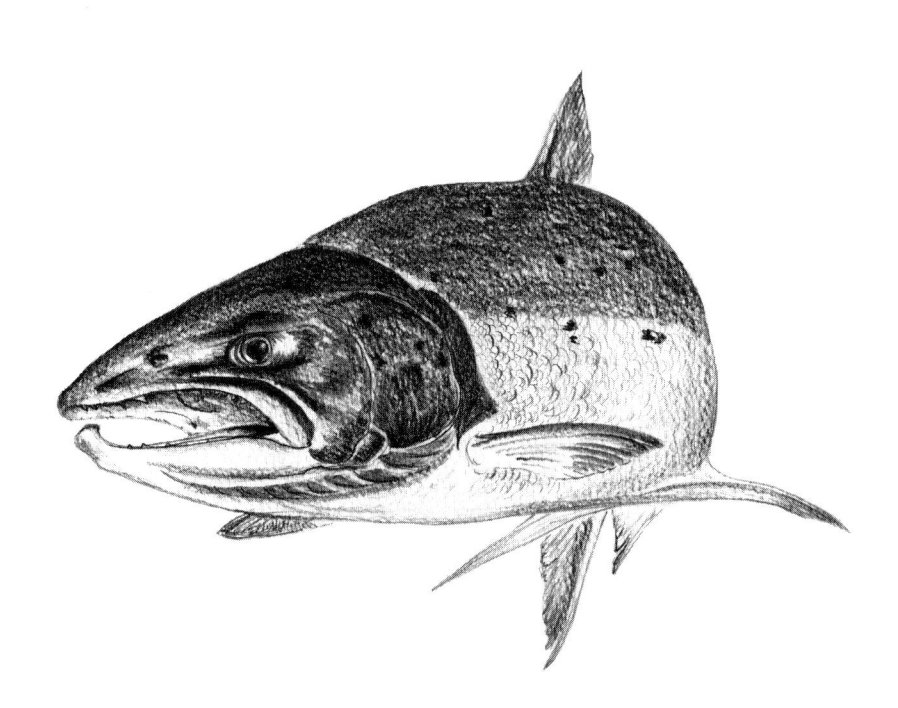

3
QUESTIONS OF BREEDING

Man has long believed salmon spawning to be a process waiting to be improved by artificial means: the fish must not be left to breed without his guiding hand – that would never do. In 1861 Charles Dickens said the French Government were developing fish culture stations and what could be done in France could surely also be done in England. In his journal *All the Year Round* he wrote of a Scottish breeding experiment:

> *It has proved that the eggs of salmon may be as carefully hatched as those of fowls and with as small a loss, while those spawned in the open river are destroyed in millions by countless natural enemies as well as droughts and spates...*

Salmon breeding on a scale described by the *Devon Weekly Times* as 'extensive' began on the Exe as long ago as 1864 when 60,000 ova (eggs) were laid down in special boxes under the supervision of a Mr Ramsbottom, son of a famous pisciculturist and himself the manager of a fish-breeding establishment in Galway. Tiverton Fishing Association were said to have been in charge of the whole enterprise. The Mayor of Tiverton and other local worthies cleared their own ponds of trout to hold these boxes and were warmly praised for their public spirit. It is interesting that the fashion then was to rear young salmon in ponds rather than streams as became the custom in later years. As long as the water was the right temperature and well oxygenated, the pond environment would have been suitable and must have seemed an ideal place. No doubt they were also encouraged by high percentage hatches of ova.

Stocking was under way in earnest on other rivers. In his *Torridge Fishery*, Lemon Gray noted that in 1866 an association at

Hatherleigh were 'turning in' fry from Thurso stock, so successfully that 'old rods' were sure they could tell the Scots at once when hooked – they fought fast but did not last, whereas the natives fought dourly and took twice as long to kill.

From the outset there was an obsession to introduce 'new blood' and for more than a century the rivers of Devon and Cornwall were stocked with millions of ova, mostly from the renowned salmon rivers of Scotland. This gave rise to an enduring belief that broad-backed, deep-sided salmon are of Scottish descent whereas those longer and thinner are 'typical Exe fish', 'typical Dart fish' and so on. That Scottish genes had shaped these differences was just assumed and proclaimed as showing that 'like breeds like'. Sceptics however wondered if ova from the spring fish of mighty Scottish rivers would still produce them if transplanted into smaller, warmer streams several hundred miles to the south. There was at least room for doubt. Now and again there were concerns too about the provenance and quality of some of the ova, there being no way of checking that they were actually from spring fish or indeed from the river named on the invoice. Some consignments looked suspiciously like bin ends.

There were several stocking techniques, each with its devotees. 'Eyed ova' (the robust stage with eyes clearly visible) were usually sent from Scotland by overnight train, packed in ice and wet moss, on muslin trays in wooden crates. They were met at the station and those surviving the journey were either 'planted' into a stream forthwith or taken to a hatchery to be reared-on. Predictably there were differing schools-of-thought about the best stage to stock: some advocating 'unfed fry', some 'feeding fry' and others parr or smolts. Ova going straight into rivers were usually just buried in what looked like suitable gravels. An alternative was to use wooden, mesh-sided (Kashmir) boxes, fixed in the flow by metal stakes driven into the stream bed. With a hinged lid so a bailiff could check progress and remove dead eggs, these were mini-hatcheries. Most had a mesh that would retain eggs but allow hatched fry to escape and fend for themselves. However, boxes of any kind were notoriously prone to being lost during spates.

All the Boards invested money and effort into stocking and faced many difficulties, some quite unexpected. The Dart Board in 1924 imported 12,000 Scottish spring fish ova at £1 a thousand, carriage paid to the nearest railway station. A carpenter made them four hatching boxes but these were soon lost during high water in the main Dart. When they persevered, using a tributary, another problem arose: the ova hatched well enough but began to die at the fry stage. Specimens were sent to a consultant naturalist who blamed the paint used on the boxes and sent them a 'recipe for a safer coating' that did the trick.

The Exe Board continued with the Scottish imports and in his 1903 Report, their Clerk summarised their situation:

> *It will be within the recollection of members of the Board that £10 has been authorised to be expended in the purchase of ova, and that an arrangement has been entered into with the Solway Fishery Co. for the supply of the same. Mr Tracey, of Exebridge... has very kindly offered... the gratuitous use of his ponds for the purpose of rearing the fish until they are able to look after themselves.*

Mr Tracey was the proprietor of a hatchery on the Exe and very willing to help the stocking crusade any way he could. For instance, in 1924 he fertilized some ova from Exe hen salmon with milt from Tay cocks sent to him in a vacuum flask through the 'kind offices' of the Scottish salmon guru, W.J.M. ('Jock') Menzies. By the following February he had 12,000 strong fry and hoping to rear some of them to smolts. He was less fortunate with milt from the Shin which failed to fertilize a single Exe ovum, a result attributed to delays in transit.

In 1930, reviewing the stocking of 40,000 Scottish ova, this Clerk voiced his misgivings. Allowing for likely losses, he reckoned any fish hooked that had come from Scottish ova could well have cost them a guinea. Might it not be wiser he asked, to spend that money on opening-up inaccessible stretches of the river and improving spawning grounds? It was brave of him to raise this fundamental point at a time when most salmon interests were convinced the only way forward was to stock Scottish ova and Boards felt left out if they were not doing so. In that atmosphere his heretical suggestion was doubtless attributed to his being of unsound mind or maybe sickening for something. Either way, the stocking continued.

Throughout the 1920s the Teign Board stocked heavily with eyed ova and yearlings from the Tay and other great rivers of Scotland but not enough to satisfy two members who started their own hatchery with a Board contribution of £5. Although their main source of ova was Scotland, they also hatched some from Teign fish taken from their spawning beds. Even in 1941, with Britain under threat of German invasion, stocking continued – vital war work in some minds and not just on the Teign.

In the 1960s another private salmon hatchery was built and run at Axminster by a local businessman to support the failing Axe. This hilltop installation at his house overlooking the river was fed by sweet water and had rearing units landscaped into a magnificent garden. Unfortunately, despite the determination of its creator and his gardener, this unique hatchery probably did little to help the Axe in the long term.

I was introduced to the mysteries of salmon stocking on my first day with the Devon Board in 1960. It had been decided that bailiffs would take the newcomer to plant ova on Dartmoor and to enrich the experience they had arranged for it to rain heavily all day. Clad in long macs, thigh boots and whatever hats we had, we were soon soaked. However, since we were to work in swollen streams, that did not matter much. With picks, rakes and shovels we excavated shallow depressions in the stream gravels, trying our best to imitate salmon redds. Bemused Dartmoor ponies came over for a look but soon lost interest. Hardy sheep coughed and grazed indifferently. A bunch of sodden cattle huddled together, moaning in chorus at the downpour. Nearby tors were faint in the gloom. It would have been a good day to break from Dartmoor Prison, never mind plant salmon ova. We laboured away and the rain kept coming. I wondered if every day would be that good. Eventually the job was done and we returned to base. I had been lucky said the bailiffs as we were drying-out – sometimes the weather could turn nasty up there. My initiation was over. For me of course, working in such weather had been a novelty but bailiffs were expected to do so whatever the weather. An annual report of the Cornwall Board illustrated the point with some style:

> *It is perhaps pertinent to mention that the decanting of the ova... coincided with blizzard conditions... but in spite of nature's vagaries the operation was successfully completed...*

Most of the ova we planted that day went into the Dart down a clear plastic tube inserted into the gravels of a tributary. To do that, one man held it aloft while another poured ova into it via a plastic funnel and washed them down with jugs of water. This method was fine but there was no way to check on the fate of the planted ova. With Kashmir boxes out of favour, a new way of planting ova was urgently needed. The bailiffs thought we had one when it was noticed that Woolworths were selling little plastic gadgets for using up scraps of soap. These had a short handle with a container at one end to take the soap and allow it to be shaken in a bath to encouraged a nice lather. At a few pence each, they also had potential for our purpose so we filled a few with ova and buried them at intervals in the gravel, leaving markers on the bank so we could find them again. The stream was rising fast as we left the scene with fingers firmly crossed. We never did know the fate of those planted via the tube but a few days later we checked the soap-shakers and were saddened to find them choked with silt and putrefying ova. Cheap hatching-boxes had really cost us dearly.

As well as importing ova, the Devon Board wanted to take some from local fish, so traps to catch spawners were installed on several rivers. At Buckfast and Swincombe, on the Dart, we used existing fish-passes as traps. At each, a basket made of angle-iron and weldmesh was made to fit snugly into one of the pools of the pass. Using pulleys we could in theory lower the basket into the pool, then haul it out when we saw a salmon jump into it. At Buckfast we tried to do so with the river in spate and every time we lowered it into the water, the force of the flow threw it back at us. Eventually we gave the river best and only fished it with the water just starting to rise after rain. For all the challenge of operating these sites, the greater burden was keeping the captives safe and sound (sometimes for several weeks) in less than ideal circumstances. For Dart fish, for example, we had to adapt disused concrete tanks at a water treatment works, which was fine except for having to carry heavy, writhing salmon in dip-nets twenty feet down a ladder to release them at water level. Snags of one sort or another were encountered at all these temporary trapping-and-holding sites and they were becoming too time-consuming for the bailiff force to run – even though nobody went home before a job was done. The solution was thought to be a permanent site capable of yielding enough ova for the whole area. The search was on.

A site was found at Beasley, on the Barle, a major tributary of the Exe. Here a disused mill had been used as a small hydroelectric station and a head of water was impounded by a weir that had a series of pools acting as a fish-pass. The disused site was acquired and adapted for the purpose by constructing large 'holding-pens' (each holding 150 salmon), one for cocks, the other for hens. Between them was a trap into which a flow of water, regulated by a sluice, would attract fish from the river via the old tailrace. It would be fished by turning down the flow but leaving about a foot of water for the fish already held. All the operator had to do was catch the newcomers in a dip-net and then 'post' them through flaps into the appropriate holding pens according to sex. Anyway, that was the plan.

To our embarrassment the river still proved more attractive and only a few fish ventured up the tailrace and into our trap. So, we had to make the fish-pass route less attractive. This we did by rigging a hanging-chain barrier across the river and then electrifying it. It took a bit of trial-and-error to get the current right. At first we had it too high and salmon approaching the chains showed their displeasure by leaping out of the water and careering madly around on their tails (who could blame them?) while we rushed to turn down the juice. We soon had enough fish avoiding the barrier and coming our way. If they were there, we could catch them. A sample of fish was examined post-mortem for any damage that might have been caused by the electric current, but nothing was found. We even compared the progeny of fish caught using electricity with those of fish not so exposed. We could detect no difference between them. Overall, the project was a qualified success: we had our one good site, but Exe salmon interests were not too keen to supply the whole area with ova from their river. Then a killer disease (Chapter 4) arrived to complicate matters further.

Before that happened, salmon were caught at these installations every autumn and held for sometimes weeks until ready to spawn. When ripe, the females were 'stripped' by hand of their ova into plastic bowls where they were fertilised with a squirt of milt from a ready male – the happy couples being chosen at random with no selection for size, shape, age, colour, or anything else. Fertilised eggs were taken to be incubated at the Board's hatchery at North Molton where bailiffs did their best to rear salmon to all stages up to and including smolts. It was not easy. The water supply, via a long leat from the Mole, was open to the weather and prone therefore to fluctuations in volume, quality and temperature. Every spate brought choking silt. Droughts reduced inflow to a trickle while cold snaps froze it solid. As well as the known threats, there was always the fear of the unexpected: a toxic spillage upstream might pollute the leat while a breach in its bank could empty it. It was far from being an ideal site for hatching and rearing salmon but we could find nowhere better in the Board's area. On reflection, our requirement for a reliable three million gallons a day of clean water at constant temperature had perhaps been a shade ambitious.

In the circumstances it is hardly surprising diseases were of constant concern. Alevins, for instance, often hatched with pinched yolk-sacs – an invariably fatal condition. Many of those lucky enough to avoid that fate, developed a bacterial gill-disease and choked to death. Some were even killed when lovingly treated with a fungicide, only later found to be available in two forms – one acutely toxic to fish. Incidents like these were hard to take and made us wonder whether, on practical grounds alone, artificial breeding was worth the effort.

Some of the fry were reared-on to yearlings and a few to smolts. The first stage was to persuade them to feed – a messy affair featuring minced liver and much patience. As soon as they were feeding freely, they were transferred outside to smolt-rearing tanks imported at considerable expense from Sweden. There they were fed mainly on high-quality pellets and some did eventually become smolts. In contrast to the early pioneers, with their preference for rearing young salmon in pools, we brought fish on in fast-flowing water to prepare them as best we could for the wild. It was a constant battle against mink, rats, kingfishers, magpies and the like in search of a meal. There was also the unexpected as when scores of pre-smolts, spooked by a low-flying jet, jumped out of their tanks and expired on the surrounding concrete. There was no advice in the literature on coping with attacks by the RAF but since our hatchery manual was American that was hardly surprising. Desperate for background reading, we even subscribed to *Progressive Fish Culturist*, a journal from the USA packed with tips for rearing channel catfish but little use at a salmon hatchery.

It was at this installation I learned to beware of the media, no matter how engaging their company or flattering their attention. At that time the BBC had a popular TV programme called *Tonight*, networked nationally, five nights a week, after the early evening news. To be featured on it was a great coup and we were delighted one day to learn they wanted to do an item on our salmon stocking. One of their famous presenters and his large support crew spent a day at the hatchery filming background, enjoying a ploughman's in the local, researching the story and so on. The Devon Board had decided I would do any interviews required, despite my lack of media training or experience (nobody had any of the former or much of the latter). After lunch the BBC decided they did want me to be interviewed by the famous presenter, so we rehearsed camera angles, voice levels and subject areas, but not questions for fear, said the director, of destroying spontaneity. My interviewer said he was ready and we began. Skilfully prompted, I muttered a few words about what we were doing and then we did it again. Next they had a little conference to one side: the interviewer nodded and turned back to me. The director said they probably had enough in the can but would I mind doing it just one more time – best to be sure and, by the way, he thought I was a 'natural'. More confidently than before, I gave similar answers to similar questions for a third time. Then, as if the point had just come to him and with the camera still rolling, the interviewer accused me of spending large sums of public money to benefit a few rich fishery owners – would I care to comment? Strangely enough, there had been not a hint of that in the pub. I do not recall my response but it cannot have been convincing. All part of the game they said, offering us beaming smiles and looking at their watches. Then quick handshakes all round and away to London.

Stocking the reared salmon was pretty hit-and-miss with persistent worries about things like air supply to and ammonia build-up in the tanks carrying them from hatchery to stream. On a hot day there was also the temperature of that stream to think about for the water in the tanks warmed-up on the journey. Crude efforts to even things up by splashing stream water into the buckets helped but the shock of being plunged into colder water killed a great many fish just when they were free to go where they pleased. Sadly it was common to see dead and dying fish as a hatchery truck departed.

The Devon Board did not usually prepare streams to receive hatchery fish. Fry were just distributed into likely pools as far from bridges as they could be carried in cans of water. It was exhausting work, a far cry from earlier days when Great Western Railway Company allowed trains to stop between stations along the Avon so fish could be stocked at otherwise inaccessible points. Perhaps their chairman fished the river, more likely they just knew good public relations when they saw it.

The Boards gradually improved their fish delivery systems technically and demonstrated some inspired improvisation. A story from the early days at the Cornwall Board's Endsleigh Hatchery illustrates the point. It was the dawn of the motor age and salmon fry were ready for planting in their waiting streams. Bailiffs had somehow managed to arrange for the use of a car to assist them in this task. Legend has it that both its doors and the front passenger seat were removed to accommodate milk-churns full of water in which the fry were carried. This contraption was then run to-and-fro on the public highway with the churns secured only by bailiffs in the back seat hanging on to them. It was tricky on steep hills and dangerous around bends but the soaked crew and cheering spectators along their routes enjoyed an hilarious day. The police turned a blind eye then but it would probably be unwise to resurrect the event without their prior approval.

The Cornwall Board developed their own version of the stocking game having in their early days conceived the notion of special 'nursery streams' into which ova, alevins, or fry would be 'decanted' securely within castles of stones made by the bailiffs. These sanctuaries were to keep out eels and other predators should there have been any left after they had electro-fished the stream to remove them before stocking. They tried but failed to build eel-proof barriers to keep out aspiring replacements for any they caught.

As in Devon, ova were either imported from Scotland or came from traps around the area. They even brought some in from Norway where it just so happened a wealthy fishery owner was fond of casting his line. They were convinced that from this 'new blood', shoals of giant Scottish and Norwegian salmon would come surging up the Tamar, brushing aside the local weaklings. They were encouraged in this belief by certain key factors: significantly, they had Endsleigh Hatchery with its sweet water at constant, ideal temperature. This handsome old thatched building in its beautiful garden setting had been built in 1898–99 by the Duke of Bedford to indulge his taste for importing exotic fish. It seemed perfect for rearing aristocratic ova from superior northern rivers.

They also had a culture of believing precise and rather splendid results. Thus was the survival of the Norwegian ova, to the fry stage, claimed as 88% and explained as being low because of their long journey. Normally figures around 99% were reported. They seemed wonderful but had more to do with pleasing the Board than recording hatchery reality. Their bailiffs knew good news was what the Board wanted, so that was what they got – something to gloat over. They were doing so much better than cruel, wasteful Mother Nature. Artificial breeding could not fail. Those closer to the action knew all it would take to kill everything in the hatchery would be for a dead frog to block its main supply pipe. Those burdened with such knowledge found the whole rearing concept rather less enthralling.

When I arrived at the Cornwall Board in 1967, stocking mania was in full swing and the futility of it eluded me for some time. We worked on doing it better, not whether we should be doing it at all and even produced a theory to justify practice. We reasoned that spawning salmon overcrowded some spawning areas with later fish digging redds into those made by earlier arrivals. Many ova must be wasted in the process. Such a shame. So we were really just taking ova that would have been lost anyway and planting them beyond the salmon's natural spawning range. It sounded plausible and, more importantly, the Board loved it.

The programme expanded and dominated the Board's fisheries work. Men operated traps and watched over ripening fish when they should have been guarding spawners on the gravels. Poachers poached virtually unhindered. However, with UDN worsening, it became almost impossible to keep trapped fish alive in the holding pens and we lost thousands before they could be stripped of their eggs. Since in the wild they just might have spawned and possibly passed on some immunity, we eased up on the stocking and it faded away... for a while.

The Board had invested their money and dreams in Endsleigh Hatchery, credited by salmon interests as having had a key role in the recovery of the Tamar as a salmon river. From 1902 to 1906 inclusive, for instance, more than a million fry were stocked in the river – almost all reared from ova from the north of Scotland. Some fry were marked by having their adipose fin (small, dorsal fin near tail) removed or clipped, enabling a few returning fish to be identified in subsequent seasons. Without doubt, in the early years of the twentieth century, the salmon in the Tamar were improving not only in numbers, condition, colour and shape, but also in the season of running the river – they were coming in earlier. Understandably, this near-miracle was widely attributed to the Endsleigh work. However a Government report in 1913, on the role of hatcheries in salmon management, discounted the part played by stocking. It argued that, bearing in mind when the fry were stocked, they could not have produced the observed improvements. More likely causes were the timely buying-out of estuarial netting rights, the provision of a fish-pass on an almost insurmountable obstruction in the lower reaches and a general easing of fish passage on spawning tributaries. Salmon interests doubtless took this with a pinch-of-salt, noting the Government was under pressure from Boards to give grants for hatchery developments around the country.

That same year Lord Clinton, referring to reported success on the Exe, told his Board (Taw and Torridge) that it would be 'a real advantage' to have a change of blood there. They agreed to spend £20 that year and the next on importing ova, starting with 20,000 from the Solway. His was the established view in 1913 and it would have been interesting to hear his verdict on the Government's report.

Sadly, Endsleigh's insoluble problem was shortage of water. There was however, close to the existing units, a nice, grassy bank awaiting development. The Board decided to expand rearing capacity and built a series of concrete raceways upon it. These might have produced thousands of smolts if there had been enough water to

51

supply them. Unfortunately, in most years, the springs ran low by May or June and stayed that way all summer. Despite a frantic, professional search, no additional water could be found. Maybe the decision to build had been taken during a winter downpour when the site can resemble a tropical rain forest, and the idea of it ever being short of water would have been beyond belief.

While some juggled with genes, others favoured managing spawning beds, it once having been customary for people living nearby to keep them clean and silt free. In 1901 letters to local papers complained this no longer happened on the Camel hence, it was said, that river's lamented decline. Correspondents calling themselves 'Fiery Brown' and 'Silver Grill' agreed that regular use of pick, rake and fork would be far better than employing more bailiffs and issuing expensive licences. A Camel Board proposal to appoint a Superintendent, at £500 a year plus horse allowance, may just have sparked this debate.

The Dart Board were renowned for messing about with their river to improve, as they saw it, the habitat of its salmon. Around 1920 they got it into their heads that the spawning beds on Dartmoor needed a good seeing-to. They rejected the offer of a consultant who, for three guineas a day, plus expenses, would have inspected them and advised on what needed to be done. They decided instead to contact two knowledgeable gentlemen: one of Princetown, the other of Hexworthy who, to judge by their rather tetchy correspondence, knew one another of old and did not always see eye-to-eye. But then, consultants often disagree.

Princetown reported that the beds did not need much doing to them. There were some large stones that could be removed and so on but a few years ago the beds had been raked so much that all the stones of a decent size had been removed leaving only gravel and sand that the first floods had washed away. On no account should that be done again. Some of the best beds in the river had been ruined by being over-raked. He had not looked below a certain point since he understood Hexworthy was attending to that. Hexworthy wrote, first making it clear that he would have nothing to do with Princetown. He offered his views which, like Princetown's, were not what the Board wanted to hear. He said he took a great interest in such matters, even in winter when most people were by their firesides. It would be tampering with nature to interfere with the spawning beds. There were plenty of good gravels available. He warned that if any work be done it must be supervised by an expert and carried out by men who had a real interest in the work and were not just there for the pay. To find such men would be very difficult. In any event, whatever was done, the floods would undo it.

Their combined advice to leave well alone did not deter the Board: they formed a committee and instructed the bailiffs to clear out abnormal growth of weed and replace washed-out gravel 'in size from walnuts to potatoes'. A couple of years later, the committee went to supervise work in progress and were so satisfied that they authorised a further £25 be spent on labour to assist the bailiffs. They recommended also that a pair of size-twelve rubber boots be obtained, not themselves having power to replace a worn-out pair without Board approval.

They also tried to improve the Dart's fish food production by having expensive ponds built on small side streams. In these they grew water weeds off which they hoped shrimps, insects, snails and so on would be washed into the river. They were never short of advice for these ventures: one consultant advocated adding bone-meal fertiliser to the river, another said put in 'meat, not weeds', so they sank bundles of bracken in pools as cover for shrimps and hoped for the best. Such projects were invariably disappointing and soon abandoned. Some fishery owners were however so eager for shrimp in their waters that, if they could not grow them, they would stock them. So it was that a Devon Board annual report recorded formal consent being given for 20,000 shrimp in each of the Axe and the Erme. If these desirable crustaceans were absent naturally, then it is highly unlikely that introduced stock would survive, let alone thrive, but that was not what some fishery owners wanted to hear.

Trying to manage spawning beds and food supplies was never as popular as the genetic approach, another example of which began in 1928 when 10,000 'early-running' salmon ova from Scotland, bought by a Mr Toogood, were hatched at Endsleigh then planted in the Plym as fry. In the spring of 1933, a number of fresh fish were seen in the river and thought to be 'the proceeds of Mr Toogood's stocking' since, in living memory, no salmon had ever entered the Plym at that time of year. The incoming fresh fish were in the 9-14lb category, typically the weight range of local four-year-old salmon that had spent two of those years in the river and the other two at sea. Amid the euphoria therefore was a snag: if the fish were from Toogood's fry, *they were five years old*. The consensus was that they *were* Toogood's fish and they were five years old because it had taken them three years (not two) in the river to grow big enough to become smolts. This was blamed not on their Scottish genes but on competition with the young of the 'late-running' Plym fish which were thought to be eating most of what little food there was. From that it was concluded that if the native 'late' stock could be destroyed, stocked 'early' fish could take their place, salmon would run in the fishing season and all would be well. The Board therefore formally resolved to eliminate the undesirable race and appointed a committee with power to act and, as noted elsewhere in this book, there is no clearer indicator of English resolve than that. This group went away to ponder and in time presented the Board with some great ideas for stopping incoming salmon. These included a high weir, electric screening, a revolving grating, or possibly some form of trap. All had severe technical limitations and would have been hugely expensive to build and maintain. There was also the awful possibility that if they merely stopped the undesirables from running the Plym, they might turn-tail and dump their unwanted spawn up some nearby, more valuable, river. There was no question about it, they had to be *destroyed*, not just deterred!

The Clerk reminded the Board how he, with another member and a bailiff, one morning in January, had killed five large salmon using just ordinary gaffs. Keep repeating that exercise and pretty soon 'the objectionable race would be practically exterminated at small expense'. The Board liked the sound of that and voted for it. Sure enough, it was not long before their bailiff was reporting just what they wanted to hear – he felt sure there were fewer late fish in the river than before. Of course, gaffing killed a few but did not exterminate the undesirables, nor did the sticks of dynamite periodically lobbed into Plym pools by impatient fishermen. The matter was still to the fore ten years later when the Clerk raised it at a lecture he attended in London given by the eminent Scottish salmon fisheries consultant, Jock Menzies. The Clerk gleefully reported that the great man had supported the attempted destruction of the late run which he thought would be 'a good thing' and the Board were delighted to have his support.

The Cornwall Board tried another way of helping the natural breeding process when it was able to create a fish sanctuary in the upper reaches of the tidal Tamar, a part of the river owned by the Duke of Bedford and practically never fished with a net. In the frequent very dry summers of the early 1900s, it was thought to be invaluable as a sanctuary for the salmon that might otherwise have been netted out. The idea took hold that it would be of great value to the stock if this 'salmon reserve' could be provided in perpetuity. In 1959 the Cornwall Board managed to acquire all the rights that mattered in roughly the upper six or so miles of tidal water, including the rare feature of private netting rights in tidal waters. The former owner had exercised that right with great restraint but who could say what might happen if in the future it fell into less scrupulous hands. So, from 1959 onwards, incoming fish could if they chose to do so, rest in the sanctuary awaiting the urge to move off up-river to spawn. So far so good, but the story did not end there. The Board had made it clear that it intended for a few years to operate its right to net commercially so as to recoup its capital outlay. It had also started to operate a trap just upstream at Gunnislake Weir for the sensible purpose of counting salmon – even suggesting it might tag a few. Then it announced that using a net might damage fish not caught and killed, so they would take fish from the trap instead. I do not know what happened thereafter but both netting and trapping ended almost before they were into their stride. They disappeared from the annual report and were not mentioned at Chaiman's Conferences when I was there. Whispers were of a Question in the House and I suspect pressure from angling interests, but research continues.

I have been disparaging about efforts at large-scale manipulation of the natural order of things but must admit to having tried to do so myself on more than one occasion. The first began in 1964 when I hatched what we called the Teign Salmon Experiment. This came about when a routine survey confirmed what the bailiffs already knew – that a large area of the Teign's high moorland headwaters, upstream of an obstruction called Manga Falls, could not be reached by salmon. There was a resident population of brown trout, sea trout spawned there and the whole area seemed highly suitable for rearing salmon. It was also reasonably certain that not even extensive blasting could have opened it up to adult salmon, there being a stretch of river a mile long that was virtually a continuous obstacle. With few exceptions, the area's trout did not reach any great size. Salmon on the other hand had only to reach a few inches long in order to become smolts and go to sea for some serious growing. The exciting idea began to form therefore that if the area could be stocked with salmon it would produce a large number of smolts (wild, or as good as) thereby boosting the Teign salmon run.

One obvious snag however was the area being already packed with brownies all poised to gorge on any introduced fry, especially those not at their best after the trip from the hatchery. When the experiment began in 1964, a vital first step therefore was to make some space for the salmon by removing as many trout as possible and 'dumping' them at points in the river downstream of Manga Falls. Fish in the receiving waters probably did not appreciate having thousands of alien trout suddenly poured into their territory but there was no other option. Killing-out the whole area with a fish toxin such as rotenone would not have been tolerated by many diverse and vociferous interests even if it had been the answer. It was intended also to keep sea trout out of the area by trapping and relocating them below the obstruction.

To give it a flying start, the Board committed an existing standing order of 50,000 Tweed ova to the project and said it would do likewise for a further five years. Also any ova from trapping sea trout would be traded for salmon ova (two trout for one salmon), probably from the Lune in Lancashire. Such was the plan and that April, in foul weather, bailiffs managed to stock 30,000 ready-to-feed fry. Unfortunately they had not travelled well from the hatchery and were described as 'very sick' when released. Their survival was understandably poor but 20,000 feeding-fry the following year did much better. In June 1966, 23,000 feeding-fry were in good condition when planted, despite being carried over three miles of very tough going. The project was going well but in 1967 unpredictable events began to affect it when repeated outbreaks of disease at North Molton Hatchery made it impossible to stock any fish from there. Disruption arising from these new circumstances (and various organisational changes) caused this project to fade into the background, where I guess it became deeply unfashionable and best let lie. However, if anyone is looking at ways to improve the Teign's salmon runs, there lies an idea worth dusting off.

A couple of years later I was pleased to hear of one interesting outcome. Apparently, trout missed in the clearance had grown as never before, delighting a select few who knew where to find them. Theory had always held that Dartmoor's trout were small because very favourable spawning conditions produced too many of them for the space and food available. Here was a practical demonstration that if they were thinned out, those remaining would put on weight. A similar effect had also been noticed on Exmoor in the aftermath of the disastrous flooding in the Lynmouth area in 1952. Many small fish from the Lyn and other local rivers had been left high and dry when the floods receded and the Devon Board reported:

> ...the destruction of numbers of small fish has restored the balance of fish to available food. The larger, stronger fish survived to the advantage of the fisheries. Fishermen are unanimous that the fish, especially as regards size, are much improved. There is no scarcity of good-sized fish or fish food.

In 1968, I was again disrupting the natural order of things and had better explain why. Fresh from my stint in western Canada and much influenced by it, I wanted to make the freshwater fishing in my new patch (the Cornwall Board's area) available to more people than it had been hitherto and I was on the lookout for any way that might be done. About the same time, the fish world and its media were full of the successful introduction of Pacific Salmon into the Great Lakes in North America and I began to toy with the notion of creating a big new public fishery with all the benefits that would bring to the area.

Not having the Great Lakes to play with nor being allowed to import Pacific Salmon ova, some adaptation of the concept was clearly called for. I took stock. What we did have were lots of small and unproductive streams flowing into bountiful coastal waters with the mighty Atlantic beyond. We also had rainbow trout, recently (with some misgivings) stocked into a few reservoirs to improve their fishing. I knew the rainbow species had a sea-going variety called a 'steelhead', with a life-story not unlike that of the salmon. It was reputedly popular with fishermen. Suppose those streams could become nurseries for rainbows which would then go to sea to grow and support a steelhead fishery in the estuaries and coastal waters. I could not wait to get going and talked the Board into a trial to see how rainbow fry would adapt to Cornish streams because they seemed to prefer still to running water from which they tended to disappear soon after stocking. With great originality I called this project the 'Rainbow Trout Experiment'.

We piloted the idea on the Valency, a tiny stream on Cornwall's north coast and, further west, on the Porth Stream, the main feeder to a small public water supply reservoir. With nets and electric-fishing gear we removed as many of their native trout and eels as possible and put them in neighbouring waters. Being sensitive souls, we again did not dare use a toxin to stun or kill fish, for fear of adverse public reaction.

We stocked the streams with several thousand rainbow fry hatched from imported Danish ova. Although there was no expectation of an actual steelhead fishery, we would have been thrilled to see even one fish. For that to happen we were relying on the wandering nature of the species to take it off to sea when it discovered it could do so. We were in effect hoping a 'spontaneous steelhead' would arise from their Danish DNA, which was not very scientific of us. We did regular checks on survival, health, growth, movements and so on of the fry noting with pride how handsome they were growing on the bugs and snails of their streams plus anything else they could find. Said their progress report:

> *Several stomachs contained partially digested slugs and one a large caterpillar. The stomach of one fish was fully distended by sixteen wheat grains and that of another by a single large earthworm.*

Unfortunately there were fewer and fewer to admire and within a year most of them had vanished. Tempting though it was to think they were at sea and would return as steelhead, we feared that was not so. Predators must have eaten quite a few; we had found one protruding, half-digested, from the mouth of a large trout and the stomach of an eel had revealed another. There were also press reports of a cormorant feeding so greedily on the Valency that it had become a tourist attraction. We did not actually *know* it was eating our rainbows but it might well have been the stocked fry on their way to the sea.

But it was human predators that worried us most. Both streams remained open to angling during the experiment although we tried to keep quiet about the removal of salmon and trout and the stocking of rainbows. This naive approach was brought home to us when two small rod-carrying boys, on holiday from London, proudly showed the crew five of our rainbows they had just taken from the Valency. Apparently, all the village knew about the stocking and bread paste had become the favoured bait. Another day a group of fishing lads eagerly showed us five more of our beauties and swore by worming. When we heard of a man who had taken thirty-seven with a spinner, we knew the dream had been temporarily set-back. It was some consolation that we had had the local kids chasing rainbows and kept them out of mischief for a while. Perhaps 8,000 rainbow fry did not vanish in vain.

There were also incidental benefits. As had been observed after the attempt to clear trout from the headwaters of the Teign and in the aftermath of the Lynmouth floods, the size and condition of trout missed during the Porth and Valency operations appeared to improve, an observation adding support to 'thinning-out' as a management option for local trout streams. Another plus related to misgivings about stocking rainbows into reservoirs and ponds in the area and concerns they might escape and threaten native fish stocks. If it had done little else, the Rainbow Trout Experiment demonstrated how hard it might be for escaped rainbows to establish themselves in Cornish streams.

I have recently had the opportunity of seeing the early records of Endsleigh Hatchery. These make it quite clear that the Duke of Bedford did his level best, over several years, to establish rainbows in the Tamar, stocking thousands of them from various sources including a first batch of 2,000 imported from America. Although he managed to get rainbows to spawn in the river, he failed to establish them there in the long term. Clearly my modest little effort was 'Rainbow Trout Experiment II' and not quite the pioneering work it had seemed to be at the time.

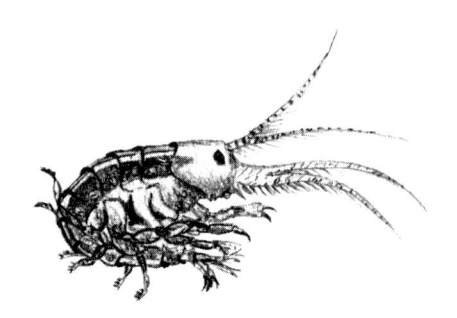

4
Plagues and Problems

In their daily existence salmon are faced with a variety of threats, some believed to be natural in origin, others thought accidentally or deliberately to be the fault of man. This chapter looks at some of the perils that have affected salmon in the South West and man's best efforts to counter them.

In 1911 an alarming disease struck the Exe, killing over two hundred salmon. Victims had ulcers on their bodies and entrails congested with black matter. Outbreaks followed on other rivers but the Exe was always the worst hit. In 1928 the same bug claimed at least a hundred salmon. A bacterial disease called furunculosis was thought to be responsible. An inflamed intestine and anal bleeding were other signs of a disease that seemed to be at its worst when rivers were low and water temperatures rising. However, despite many hot summers, there have been no major outbreaks since – the stock presumably having acquired some immunity. Apart from counting and disposing of dead fish, there was not much that could be done.

Boards used to monitor for the bug that caused the disease although there was little to do with the results but file them and notify the Ministry. Bailiffs finding a newly-dead salmon were asked to take blood from it for examination by the Public Health Laboratory Service. Samples were held in small, screw-topped bottles. One bailiff of the old school would never produce any from his area (the upper reaches of the Dart) working on the sound principle that if there were no samples there could be no bad results. I persuaded him to take some – or so I thought. Several weeks later, on a glorious hot June morning, we met by the Dart to discuss a coming survey. I sensed straight away something was afoot. Although he never used eau de toilette, after-shave and the like (he said poachers would smell him) he was no stranger to soap and not noted for body odour. I was aghast therefore to realise that he was exuding a sickening stench. Without a word he handed over four sample bottles, within which gas fizzed from what had once been blood. He explained that he had been collecting them as requested but it had been hard to find dead fish to sample. He had not risked posting those because he wanted to be sure I got them and everyone knew what the post was like. Something told me to leave it at that.

In the late 1960s another lethal disease reached the area, the first outbreak of which had been in 1964 in County Kerry in the Irish Republic. This deadly Irish Fish Disease then 'jumped' across to the Solway Firth, spread in all directions and became known as Ulcerative Dermal Necrosis, or UDN for short. In the South West it was first noticed on the Taw and Torridge in 1968 but within a couple of years it was killing thousands of salmon all over the area. A typical early sign of trouble was the appearance of small, grey patches on the top of a fish's head which progressively became enlarged and ulcerated. Similar areas would develop on its body, especially around the bases of the fins. Fungus would flourish on the exposed wounds. Affected fish were easy to spot and became a common sight. They were usually disinterested in anglers' lures. The disease hit hardest in cold weather, especially at spawning times. Netsmen caught very few diseased specimens. Sometimes apparently clean fish, fresh-in from the sea, were badly affected. Spring runs throughout the area were devastated.

In Cornwall, the Camel was visited by something identical to UDN which for three years had to be called River Camel Fish Disease until a man from the Ministry gave it official UDN status. It killed thousands of salmon, many as they were preparing to spawn. There were peaks of mortality, often in the coldest weather, as in January 1970 when 133 dead salmon were removed in four days. An unusual aspect of this outbreak was that many smolts also died, most of them displaying a strange triangular-shaped bib of fungus under their lower jaw. Not to be outdone, the Tamar had its own special feature in that some of its salmon with signs of UDN appeared also to be developing on their heads and bodies large patches of a bluish-grey film. The Ministry would not call this UDN either and it enjoyed brief notoriety as the Tamar Blue Film Disease. It is hard to imagine it today, but those were days of minimal media interest in the environment and we had not expected our press release on the subject to attract much attention. We firmly believed in letting people know what was happening so we mentioned that affected fish were behaving in an abnormal manner and were astonished next day to find in a national daily the headline, 'Crazy Fish Riddle Probed By Scientists'. We had clearly caught them on a slack news day and our Chairman was not a bit impressed with the suggestion that fish in his area were mentally disturbed.

UDN was almost certainly a fresh outbreak of a disease previously experienced in the closing years of the nineteenth century. In that plague, fish developed ulcers and had a peculiar fungal growth described as like a 'white night-cap'. A Ministry report for 1885 said the disease (which first appeared in 1877) was 'abating in its virulence', the rivers of Devon and Cornwall being 'exempt' except for three diseased fish from the Plym. In 1886 it was reported to be 'very bad' in the Avon but the Plym was only slightly affected with no fish having died. In fact the first dead salmon were removed from the Plym on 10 January 1886 and during the next two months bailiffs buried a further 123. Some were sent for examination to the Ministry in London where they were thought to be suffering from a disease they were calling Saprolegnia (the fungus involved) although there were doubts that that had killed them. Ministry advice was that nothing could be done except to bury dead fish away from the river with an application of carbolic acid.

The Tamar and Plym Board's Superintendent had strong views on the cause of the disease. He pointed out that a field in the Plym's middle reaches had been dressed with tons of rotten fish, fish offal, foul shellfish and town refuse. When it rained, the wash from this lot ran off into the river and was the likely culprit. He believed the weather was also implicated. From early January to mid-March there had been a severe frost and piercing easterly winds. The river had begun to dry up and salmon were having difficulty spawning. The Super felt this 'delay in their work' had impaired their health and the cock fish particularly had begun to succumb to the disease.

The disease seemed to peak around 1890 but the jitters it caused lingered on. In 1902 a Fisheries Inspector was summoned from the Ministry in London to investigate an outbreak of fungus affecting dace in the lower Tamar, the Board's concern being undoubtedly for their salmon. The visitor walked the affected length with the Chairman and a bailiff, saw that only dace were showing the fungus and recovered one for 'detailed microscopical examination'. He then departed and wrote a splendid report identifying the fungus and suggesting that mine discharges to the river were somehow implicated and would bear investigation. His emphasis on the need for more work showed he would have made a fine consultant. However the lab work was no fun and the trip no 'jolly' even though (with the dace in his case) he likely had a whole carriage to himself on the train home. His report added flavour:

> *Owing unfortunately to the exigencies of travel the fish became partially decomposed... I was however able to identify the fungus as that form of Saprolegnia which is commonly known as the 'salmon disease fungus'. Although... the water in which the specimen was kept had become putrescent it was interesting to see that, even on the tenth day after, actively mobile zoospores were active in it.*

The UDN and Saprolegnia outbreaks were probably the result of virus infections but there is still doubt in both cases. Indeed, not everyone believed that UDN was a disease. Some thought the characteristic ulcers were an allergic reaction to a new irritant in the river waters. Comparisons were drawn with human skin conditions and their causes. Washing-up liquids and washing powders were prime suspects. Toxic secretions from mutant bacteria and algae were postulated. Even sunburn was suggested, just as it had been blamed for killing Bovey sea trout in the drought of 1959. Some speculated that UDN ulcers were actually radiation burns suffered by contact with dumped nuclear wastes. Others blamed secret underwater atomic explosions. However, none of these doom-laden theories would fit all the known facts.

There was much fussing over what could be done. Anglers were asked to disinfect boots and tackle before fishing an unaffected river. Some complied but many did not. Canoe events, raft races and otter hunts were cancelled. Fishing seasons were sharply curtailed. Suspicion fell on mink and eels as likely carriers, but nobody could think of what to do about it if they were. Barriers were proposed and some constructed to keep infected fish at bay. Dotty remedies were advocated, one being that entire rivers be disinfected with the

GUARDIANS OF THE SALMON

The famous giant salmon (61¼lb) taken from the Exe nets on 18 March 1924, with captor Dick Voysey and friends (by kind permission the Topsham Museum Society).

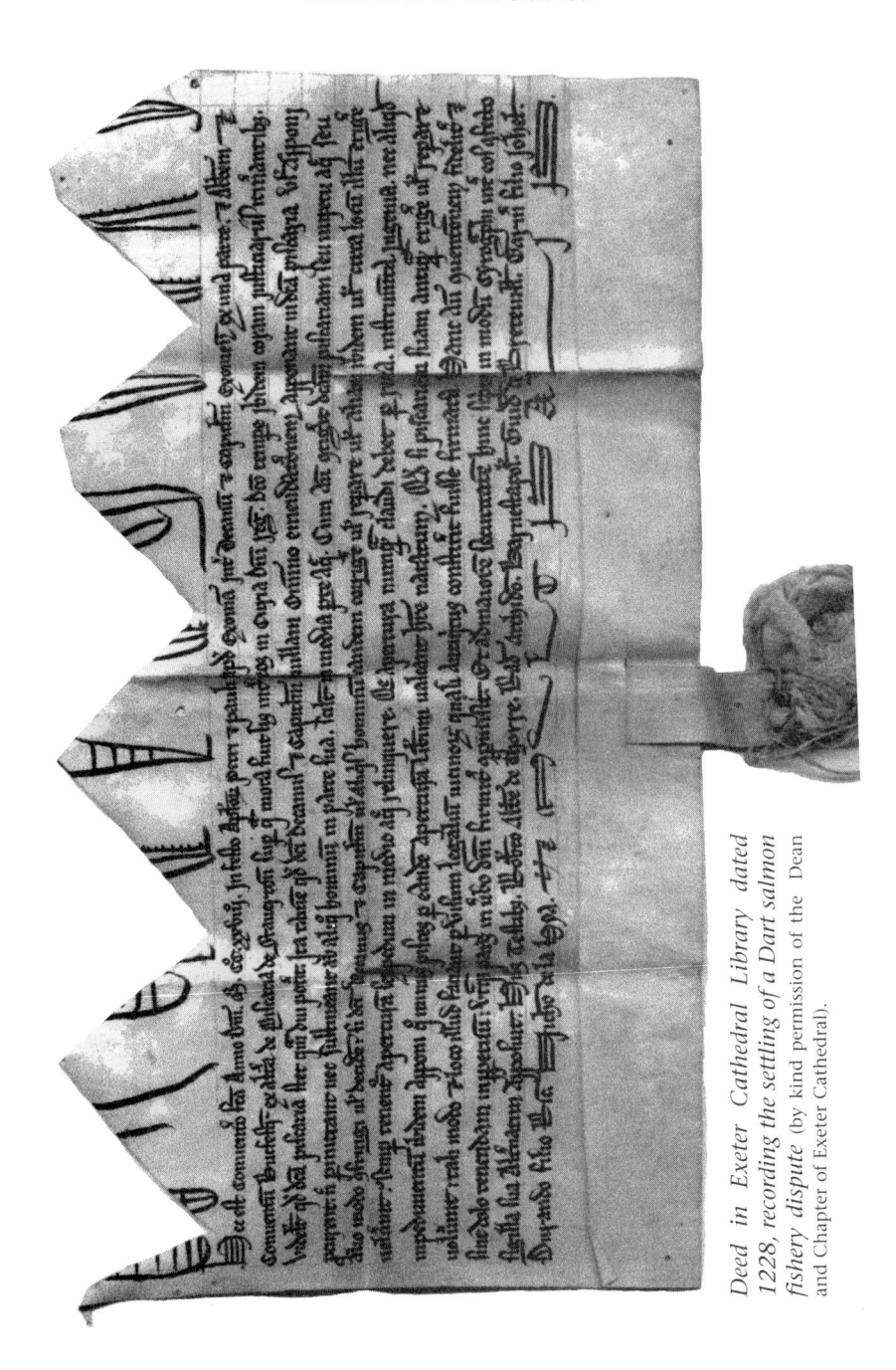

Guardians of the Salmon

Deed in Exeter Cathedral Library dated 1228, recording the settling of a Dart salmon fishery dispute (by kind permission of the Dean and Chapter of Exeter Cathedral).

GUARDIANS OF THE SALMON

Thought to have been from two hauls of net a Shaldon these 89 salmon, totalling 870lbs, were taken from the Teign Estuary, May 1922. Some fish escaped. Fishermen in the photo are believed to include Messrs Nathan (3), Jarvis, Leyman, Campbell, Shaxter and Belton. Postcards were made from the original photo.

Guardians of the Salmon

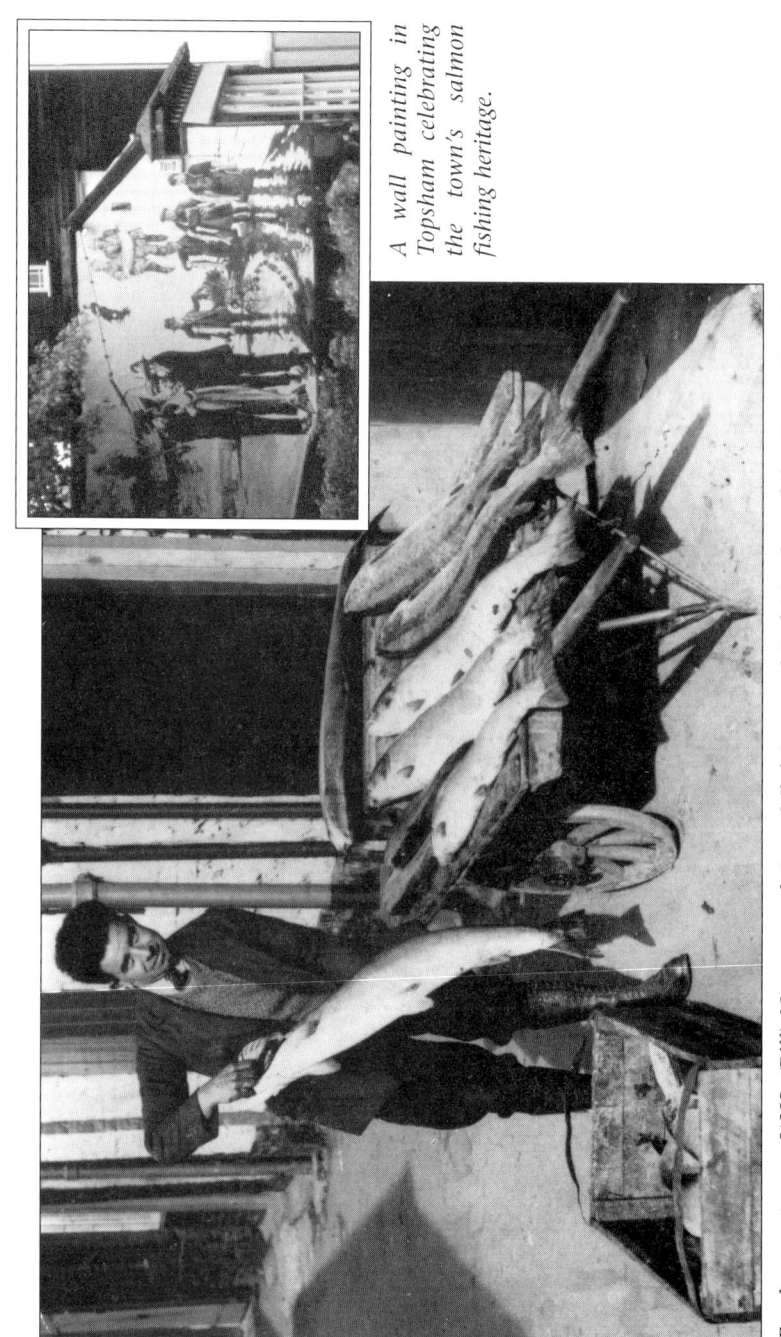

A wall painting in Topsham celebrating the town's salmon fishing heritage.

Topsham netsman W.H. (Bill) Newman – later a Ministry-appointed Member of the Devon Board – pictured here in 1934 carting salmon to the railway station for a halfpenny a pound.

GUARDIANS OF THE SALMON

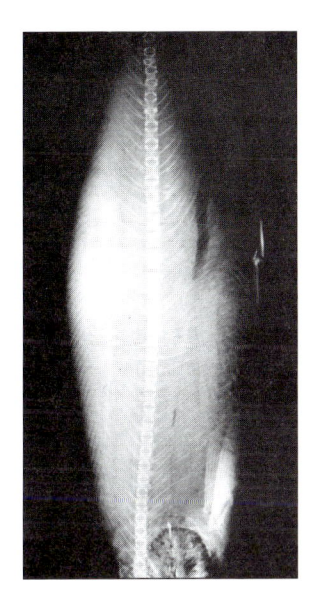

A photograph of a deformed Atlantic Salmon – initially mistaken for a Humpback salmon following large-scale stocking of that species in Russia. The x-ray (above left) shows the backbone of a normal fish, and (above right) a deformed fish.

Guardians of the Salmon

Endsleigh Hatchery on the Tamar about 1908, built 1898–99 by the Duke of Bedford. Inset: detail of a salmon trap built on the Barle in the 1960s.

A salmon trap in a fish-pass at a water intake on the upper Dart.

Above: Looking upstream at the Salmon trap on the Barle where an electric chain barrier has been suspended on the first weir of the fish-pass – early 1960s.

Left: Planting salmon fry on the upper Exe c.1964.

Guardians of the Salmon

Bailiffs gathered by the message scrawled by frustrated poachers in North Devon.

fungicide malachite green. Another proposed that all incoming salmon be intercepted, the diseased ones killed and the remainder injected with antibiotic before being released.

From the outset, a policy of removing diseased fish for burial well away from the rivers seemed to be sensible despite access to farm land being severely restricted by an outbreak of foot-and-mouth disease. Sites for mass disposal were identified but never used. Infected Area Orders were made prohibiting the movement of live fish and fish eggs. Authority was given to Boards to remove dead and diseased fish from waters 'by all suitable means'. In time the futility of it all sank in and dead fish were just left to rot in their river. Sick but still living fish were left alone in the hope they might manage to spawn and pass on some resistance. There seemed nothing else to do while Mother Nature reminded man who was really in charge of the natural world.

At the time of writing (2001) large parts of the area featured in this book are suffering from an outbreak of foot-and-mouth disease affecting cattle, sheep and pigs. It is being countered by mass culling. Sickening (and probably enduring) TV pictures of the disposal, by burning or burying, of hundreds of thousands of carcasses have been beamed around the world and there is understandable misery in the countryside. It is to be hoped there is never a simultaneous major outbreak of the disease with one affecting wild salmon stocks. It very nearly happened in 1967 which would have been bad enough but in today's media glare it would likely cause a major environmental panic.

A mysterious salmon ailment came to my notice in 1961 when the Devon Board asked fishermen to watch out for Humpback salmon (a Pacific species) that might appear in local waters following massive stocking in northern Russia. In March of that year there was great excitement when a fish caught on the Exe was thought at first to be a Humpback. Sadly (we were curious to see one) it turned out to be one of ours with an abnormal swelling beside its dorsal fin. A few more were caught in the Exe and there was one taken in the Taw. All had fusion and compression of spinal vertebrae in the swollen area, yet the flesh of the swelling itself appeared to be normal with no inflammation. There was speculation that the fish had been injured as smolts by the then new technique of electric-fishing or during their passage through turbines. More likely the deformities were a congenital condition affecting a small percentage of the population. Staff at an Exeter hospital took X-ray plates and pondered on possible links with similar human afflictions. An interested doctor wondered if at the alevin stage a yolk-sac was late being absorbed, the extra weight of it might damage the developing spine and give rise to the condition. No firm conclusions were reached and no Soviet salmon defected to local waters... that I know of.

Various interesting parasites have been found inside the area's salmon. For instance, a white blob of a creature (an inch long and the thickness of a pencil) may be encountered when a fish is cut open. A keen bailiff used to find them in dead fish he came across while patrolling the Teign. A parasitologist identified them as the larvae of a tapeworm, the adults of which were known only from fish of the sharks and rays family – the blobs were destined to stay blobs unless the salmon they were in was eaten by such a fish. Their occurrence was perfectly natural and no threat to their hosts. I wrote to the British Museum asking them to certify identification and advise me as to whether the finding of the blobs should be reported to a scientific journal. It was indeed a 'plerocercus of the tetrarhynch *Hepatoxylon trichiuri*' they confirmed, a common parasite not worth reporting – and we had thought it new to science.

Salmon may also harbour in their innards large numbers of tiny 'thread worms' a fact brought home to me one morning when a lady telephoned in great distress. Her husband had been out fishing the previous evening and not returned until late. As he often did, he had slit open his catch – she said it was a small salmon – and left it overnight on the draining board. He had now left for work, but she had just been into the kitchen and found the fish to be covered in writhing, white, inch-long threads. She was on the verge of dialling 999. My assurance that the 'disgusting things' were harmless did not help. Fish was off in that household and likely the husband too before the day was out.

Although the Devon Board let me indulge an interest in deformed salmon, Teign blobs and so on, there was no laboratory to work in until we moved from former chicken huts in Exeter to offices in a grand new County Hall built to house the legions of Devon County Council. By being vague at the planning stage about its true purpose, I managed to acquire a room with a bench and sink that would never otherwise have been allowed. Once operational however it soon became apparent that our fishy business did not sit well in their new building. Trouble centred on the corridor and stairs along which dead and sometimes decaying salmon had to be carried. The inevitable blood and slime on polished floors posed a hazard for the high-heeled and challenged the cleaners. The whiff of old cormorant heads – a connoisseur's delight – was also now and then abroad. It was ironic that I had left for a spell in Canada before the matter came to a head.

Down the years the ever-growing demands of mankind have damaged the rivers in which the salmon lived and in some of them brought the species to the brink of extinction. Toxic and smothering discharges of sewage, mine wastes, industrial effluents and the like caused serious pollution and in 1860 the Salmon Commissioners heard evidence that the rivers were in an appalling state. When they asked a director of an Exeter gas company if anything was discharged to the Exe, he spoke openly of 'deleterious refuse', including sulphuric acid, being let out twice daily as a matter of course. They were disinclined to stop this because of the cost of alternative disposal. There was also a paper mill regularly releasing the caustic liquor from bleaching straw – the raw material for paper making – making the river 'white, like soap suds' and killing fish for miles downstream.

Although many citizens were concerned, they were anxious not to upset manufacturers for fear of jeopardising jobs and a strong lobby urged a cautious approach. But a much respected industrialist, who was also Mayor of Tiverton, disagreed. He told the Commissioners he had the gas works under control as well as his factory and 'with moderate care and trifling outlay' any manufacturer could 'prevent injury' to local streams. Little had been achieved however when in

1873 an Inspector of Salmon Fisheries from the Ministry visited Exeter, had a look at the Exe and reported it to be dreadfully polluted:

> *Sewers were pouring out their horrible contents into the river, the bottom of which was a mass of foetid mud from which bladders of gas were continually rising and in which were dead dogs and cats innumerable. I was informed that big fish kills occurred each summer and on Christmas Day it seemed as if all the mills had opened their mouths and vomited forth all they possibly could for the whole of the day.*

The Salmon Commissioners heard that all the fish in the Erme had been destroyed that very year by tar from a gas works. Regular fish kills also occurred in that river, caused by effluent from a paper mill, but the witness felt sure it was released by factory workmen without the owner's consent – the poor were getting the blame as usual.

In his 1889 lecture to the Torquay Natural History Society, Webster expressed his disgust at raw sewage in the Teign, believing someone took 'iniquitous pleasure' in letting the foul stuff out on the incoming tide rather than the ebb, thus extending its effect. He complained also that tin mines on the river sent down tons of choking sand that had to be dredged out lower down at great expense. 'A few settling ponds' he lamented 'is all that is required'.

Metalliferous mining had long been a major curse of rivers in the area, being the source of poisonous effluents and vast tonnages of suffocating sand and gravel. In 1907 a Government report explained the Fowey's worst season on record for salmon and sea trout:

> *The bottom of the river... is so thick with mine sand that if the mine never sent in more it would take several years to make it fit for use by spawning fish.*

The Salmon Commissioners heard much about the effects of mining. On the Teign, a lead mine was discharging mine water with deadly effect. A local doctor told them of a kill of hundreds of salmon in 1856, some having been brought to his house for sale at four pence a pound. Fifty years earlier, he used to catch hundreds of trout in a day's fishing and now his average was seven. Things were definitely not what they used to be. In 1859 a correspondent to *Trewman's Exeter Flying Post*, writing as 'Piscator', bemoaned the wholesale destruction of Teign salmon by mine water. Even while writing his letter, someone had been at his back door offering to sell him some.

In 1868 the Lynher was killed out by mine refuse let go at the rate of a hundred tons a week. That same year, the *Western Daily Mercury* reported a disaster on the Tavy when the pumping out of the Lady Bertha mine had resulted in thousands of fish being 'most wantonly killed'. In 1871 the whole of the Tavy was poisoned again, that time by mundic (arsenical pyrites) and salmon were virtually absent from it for thirty years.

The Tavy had recovered by 1921 when there was a series of mysterious fish kills around Tavistock. For once, pollution from mines and factories was ruled out. The Tamar and Plym Board's Clerk explained that the cause was gas given off from a substance wilfully placed in the river to destroy fish. He knew what the chemical was but thought it unwise to name it in public. Suspicion fell on people protesting at increased fishing licence duties. The Clerk said those responsible were not only risking prison with hard labour but, should their names be revealed, they would be severely dealt with by those whose animals had been put at risk by the poison. That threat to name names seemed to put an end to the affair.

It was mining that for decades did terrible damage. Even so, some of those most affected seemed relaxed about it. In 1905 a member reported to the Dart Angling Association that the discharge from a Dartmoor mine had turned the river from 'sweet and clean' to 'a mahogany colour with a nasty, slimy film on top'. He knew 'no more saddening and maddening feeling than when a man saw such an unjustifiable act'. Yet he proposed 'a little quiet pressure, in a conciliatory spirit' as the action to take. Years later the same association tried a similar tack when paper mills were said to be ruining the river. The poor old Dart had apparently turned 'red, blue and green by turns', four times in ten days, prompting the newspaper headline 'River of Many Colours'. For all that, the proposition was merely that a round-robin be sent to factory owners on the river suggesting something be done.

The early Boards especially were ill-equipped to conserve the environment and industry did pretty well as it pleased. Wealth creation and jobs took priority. With few exceptions, firms were loath to incur what they saw as non-essential costs to keep rivers clean – probably not seeing the point of doing so. It should not be assumed either that the Boards were supported when they tried to safeguard the salmon, a point made by a letter to the *Tiverton Gazette* in 1900 from 'Isaaz Walton' (presumably a pseudonym). The correspondent first had a go at the Exe Board – 'a fussy and meddlesome body' – for charging him half-a-crown to fish when it had once been free. His complaint was that, prompted by the Board, the Board of Trade wanted to stop the Council building a dam across the Exe to provide water for an electric-light plant that would be much cheaper than a steam alternative. They were also trying to force the owners of the town's lace factory (employer of hundreds of people) to make an opening in their existing weir, where there had never been one before. The writer was furious that jobs were at risk. 'Bread first, then fish' was his slogan, to which he added:

> *It matters little whether a favoured idle few shall have more salmon in the upper Exe, but it does emphatically matter that those who toil and spin shall prosecute their labour unhindered.*

Although their powers were limited, Boards used to visit factories and mines, take samples for analysis and try for improvements by persuasion. They were not always welcome and in 1907 the Clerk of the Tamar and Plym Board had to report to members that he and a bailiff had been refused access and threatened with expulsion by force from a mine on the Tavy. Even in the 1960s, inspectors could expect hostility from a works manager when they went to see him about a discharge. I recall once at a plant on the Teign confronting the boss with a bottle of filthy effluent I had just taken from his outfall. Unconcerned, he told me to clear off and let those who had a proper job to do get on with it, an attitude endorsed a century earlier by the Salmon Commissioners who made a policy statement so final that acceptance of it was probably a pre-condition of their inquiry. They said:

> *...the interests of manufactures, nationally considered, must be deemed paramount to those of fisheries...*

If industrialists were bad, they had no incentive to improve by copying local authorities. With few exceptions, the urban and rural district councils had an appalling attitude towards waste treatment. 'No votes in sewage' was a slogan that identified the cause. Certainly some urban areas were served by impressive treatment works with manager, chemist, laboratory and so on, where civic pride could blossom and councillors boast to the media that the final effluent was drinkable. Far more typical were the many small plants serving rural areas, some so badly maintained as to be in effect abandoned. To take final effluent samples from them, as was my duty, required a sense of adventure, tools for clearing a path and a compass. When located, such plants were usually those at which liquid sewage, sprayed from rotating pipes, was allowed to trickle through a filter-bed of stones on which a film of bugs was feeding on the sewage particles and thereby cleaning it. Upon these rocks and their living coating rested the entire, miraculous, treatment process. It was a particular shock therefore one day to run into a workman at one works, happily shovelling the stones out of the filter in the belief that they were getting in the way of the flow of sewage. It was not that gentleman's fault that he did not understand the process. The blame lay back at the council offices with whoever was responsible for waste treatment. These were usually senior officials who, despite their lack of interest in them, resented any criticism of their works. It was customary to send results of effluent analyses to them with comments about the state of the works when the sample had been taken. Furious would be the response if it was suggested that settlement tanks needed attention or filter arms had stopped rotating. Samplers, they insisted, must confine themselves to what came out of outfall pipes and that had to be the official order of the day.

At times, pollution came from unpredictable sources such as disused mines. For example, mines can still inflict terrible damage long after they have ceased production. This happened on the Teign in 1962 when a corroded pipe in a former settlement lagoon at a disused mine, burst and released half a million gallons of a toxic brew that killed all fish and river-life for miles downstream. Adult fish apart, there were too many dead fry to count so with a team of bailiffs I estimated the damage by picking up all dead fish in sample areas. We reckoned over a hundred thousand fry had been lost, many of them being young salmon.

It was depressing to work on big fish kills, but there were lighter moments. One came when I failed to find those guilty of killing fish along a couple of miles of the Erme when suspicion had fallen on a new, supposedly harmless, weed killer recently used to spray road verges in Ivybridge. Despite snooping around the town flashing my warrant, I could find nothing to support my hunch that cans of older, toxic stock had been used. The pathologist's report on the dead fish was inconclusive and the case had to be closed. When I explained this to the Devon Board, a reverend member, who was also on the county's police committee, spluttered that the police could always determine cause of death when a body was found, so why could not we do the same for fish? My spur-of-the-moment response that the police could at least question the deceased's friends and relatives, was not appreciated.

The Salmon Commissioners heard how mining had damaged salmon runs in Cornwall where the Camel and Fowey were virtually fishless. A local MP said the 'evils of the river' had begun in the early 1800s. He had been out fishing as a boy when the foul water had first come down the river and killed all the fish. As mining expanded, the poisoning had worsened. A fisherman from Fowey said the coloured mine water was still visible in the sea two miles out.

With the MP and a Mr Deeble Boger, an expert witness, there was discussion as to whether anything could be done. Consideration was even given to cutting, parallel to the river, a new channel some twenty miles long to take mine wastes direct to the sea. The main obstacle to this was not the engineering challenge but the legal worries of having a channel full of poison running through so much private land.

It was something that they were discussing it, for the prevailing Cornish attitudes seemed to be that salmon were there to be killed and rivers were cheap, natural drains. The MP declared that against mining, 'fishing must sink into utter insignificance' and in their report the Salmon Commissioners reflected:

> ...to prefer the salmon rivers of Cornwall, which indeed are not of the first class, to the great mining interests that form the staple industry of that wealthy county, would be to preserve salmon at a preposterous cost.

Early in the twentieth century, with the coming of motorised transport, there was concern that tar, then being used on roads for the first time, might in wet weather be releasing toxic chemicals into the rivers. The Boards agonised but failed to discover evidence of harm which of course is not to say no harm was being done. In fact a Ministry committee concluded that certain constituents of tar were lethal to fish and their food organisms. They established that tar was at its most dangerous after application, before it had set, and showed also that silt in the water somehow made tar washings more toxic. Another curse coming with motor vehicles was the casual disposal of their used oil down drains leading to the rivers. In 1939 the Clerk of the Tamar and Plym Board reported a special problem arising with lorries as a consequence of a new Diseases of Animals Act which required the cleaning and disinfection of vehicles that had conveyed cattle. They had to be scraped, washed and treated with quick-lime which was fine except they were then being driven into rivers and the whole mess washed away in the flow. The 'litter' from the process could be seen at considerable distances downstream and the Clerk reported that he had passed the matter to the police.

By the 1960s, worries about tar and oil had given way to new ones such as acid rain, pollution from farms, changes in land use and so on. Causing particular anxiety was the widespread draining of wet land to bring it into production. This was seen by many as removing the upland 'sponge' from rivers, causing rain to run-off in silt-laden spates where previously levels had risen and fallen steadily with less colour in the water. Such changes were thought to be altering the pattern of salmon movements and shortening the time when conditions were best for rod fishing. That was bad news for anglers and a largely unheeded warning that increasing siltation would in time pose a major threat to the salmon.

Another came from the Boards themselves when their land drainage departments followed Ministry policy to improve agricultural land. Being good engineers they did not mess about and began to use heavy earth-moving plant on rivers such as those in East Devon. From a fisheries standpoint, these works eliminated desirable pools and bank-side vegetation and devastated fish habitat generally, while the sight of bulldozers working in their beloved waters threatened the hearts and minds of fishermen. Worse still, the works needed regular maintenance as natural forces worked to restore their former state.

Whatever the rationale, it had been the engineers' misfortune that they encountered a group of fishery owners already at the end of their tether over the Axe Trap, a Ministry research station of supreme unpopularity. This had been built across the river's lower reaches to intercept all fish, moving upstream or down, so they could be counted, measured and have a few scales removed. Some also had identity tags attached to their bodies before being released. Axe anglers were convinced the stress and injury of these procedures made fish impossible to catch and condemned many to die within days. The enraged fishery owners tried desperately to have this hated trap closed down, but the Ministry would not be moved. When all else had failed, wild rumours began to circulate that a group of ex-military gentlemen were planning direct action. They were said to think that all it would take to be rid of the offensive fence would be a small charge of dynamite floated down to it by night from upstream. There would be a loud bang and the hated structure would be spread in small pieces over an area of East Devon. Simple. Unfortunately reconnaissance showed there to be an operator on duty at all times and they drew the line at the risk of blowing him into the next field – even thwarted salmon fishermen had limits. I have no proof that this story was ever seriously in anyone's mind, but I heard the rumours myself. Maybe it was just good for them to consider how it *might* be done, if only... .

Various unexpected, transient threats have faced the guardians of the salmon. For instance, in the years leading up to the First World War, the exploding of practice torpedoes in the Tamar estuary caused concern to the Tamar and Plym Board who thought them responsible for a number of blind salmon turning up in fishing nets. Coming war or not, negotiations with the Navy had the firing area moved and there were no more sightless fish.

Hostilities over, the Board objected to a scheme to divert water from high areas of Dartmoor to generate hydroelectricity, ostensibly a good thing, but bad for the salmon. Plans were then revived for industrial-scale peat working on the Moor. The Board believed extensive removal of peat would damage the rivers in the area to be worked. Resolving strongly to oppose the plan, they must have reflected that if their experience was any guide there would never be any shortage of ingenious proposals to threaten the salmon.

An example was an ambitious plan for building a reservoir on the high cliffs of North Devon, linked by massive pipes to the sea far below. In times of low electricity demand, sea water would have been pumped up into the high reservoir to be held for discharge through turbines to generate instant power when demand required it. There was considerable relief when this 'pumped storage' scheme was dropped, there being a belief in some quarters that salt water might have leaked from the 'head pond' and found its way to the headwaters of the Torridge.

A more conventional threat was posed by a power station proposed for the Tamar estuary. Not unreasonably the then Central Electricity Generating Board argued that since the South West was happy enough to use power imported down the National Grid, it would be only fair that it also have a generating station in the area. This view was not met with universal joy and there ensued a public inquiry at which opposing sides exchanged fierce and expensive fire. There were concerns about so-called 'stack emissions' that it was said would cause acid rain to fall on nearby Dartmoor. There were worries also that fish would be killed in the turbines or be distracted by the huge volume of cooling-water that would have to be discharged. The CEGB had a first-class team of scientists and engineers, aware of such problems and ready with reasonable answers to them. Opponents of the development were however growing generally more cynical and less likely to accept official assurances and a quick fix was out of the question. However, unless they built it when my back was turned, there is so far (2001) no sign of this generating station – maybe the circumstances have changed.

By the late 1950s an apparently insoluble dilemma was fast coming to the fore. To thrive, salmon needed plenty of cool, clean water, but people demanded it too in ever increasing volumes for uses both trivial and vital. As the Boards went out of existence, the search was on for more and more millions of gallons a day to be made available for human use.

Traditionally man used to raid the uplands for water long before Boards to protect salmon were thought of. When the Dart Board used to send working-parties to Dartmoor to inspect leats coming off the Dart, it was the water supply legacy of centuries that confronted them. There was little they could do about those superbly engineered channels that were invariably diverting millions of gallons a day of sweet Dart water to Plymouth, leaving behind residual trickles in the streams from which they flowed. It is doubtful that admiring the engineering featured much in the working-party's programme for the day.

Direct abstraction however was eventually inadequate for man's needs in the drier times. As I write, rain has been hammering against my windows for hours: fields are awash, rivers are in flood. It was like this yesterday and will be again, if not tomorrow, then in a day or so. More than enough water falls from the sky but in the Boards' era not enough was stored for drier times. Strategic lakes were needed but the water management arrangements in place led instead to the promotion of more local solutions to the problems.

The Boards, with their inadequate finance and weak powers, were ill-equipped to make much of a stand for salmon when the search was on for more water. Negotiations must have been difficult when, for instance, in 1927 Torquay Corporation wanted to take water direct from the Teign near its Dartmoor source. The Teign Board accepted £1,000 and a set of rules aimed at minimising the damaging effects of the abstraction. They wisely invested the money in two new fish-passes miles downstream to improve fish passage and help natural spawning compensate for any lost production in the headwaters. Unfortunately, a few years later, they took an inadequate £250 for 'loss of spawning beds' when this direct intake was replaced by a reservoir that would deprive the salmon of miles of prime spawning area. There were such deals done on other rivers as the Boards fought to squeeze as much cash as they could out of each proposal.

So fragile was their financial position that even the most unlikely income must have been a godsend. It was common practice for a trickle of 'compensation water' to be released from a reservoir to try and preserve some life downstream of it. In 1940, following a dry summer, the reservoir supplying Plymouth dropped to a very low level. There being a war on, it was thought prudent to conserve water in case of fires after bombing raids, so the compensation flow was turned off and the Board were paid £1 a day while the arrangement lasted.

There was little love lost between the Boards and the various water undertakers and fierce squabbles used to break out about whether, for example, compensation water was actually being released as agreed. Gauges would mysteriously err and valves unexpectedly jam, by some law of water engineering, *never* in favour of the river. Put simply, water engineers regarded flows released or protected for fisheries purposes as a complete waste of water and did their utmost to get around the few rules that existed.

In 1963 the Boards were given responsibilities for water resources. Within a decade large regional projects were afoot with greatly increased storage to back up abstractions from the rivers. Measures were agreed to safeguard as far as possible the fisheries of affected rivers. Costly research was proposed to monitor the effects of abstraction and promises extracted to rectify any damage so discovered.

This however was not enough for some who believed nothing could compensate for the disturbance of the natural order that would inevitably occur. Once, being cross-examined at a public inquiry into a proposed reservoir and abstraction scheme, I was making the best of a planned hatchery, when sharply interrupted by my interrogator, a renowned local solicitor. What I was saying was all very well, he said, but really the river would be devastated and efforts made to mitigate the damage were just futile. My role, he put it to me, was akin to being the landscape architect to 'Bomber Harris' (who directed the RAF's saturation bombing of German cities during the Second World War). Not surprisingly, the normally stuffy proceedings dissolved into laughter and cheers for a fair point, memorably made.

Guardians of the Salmon

5
Trouble at Mills

Erection of a weir or trap on a salmon river usually meant trouble not only for the fish, but for the structure's owners and operators and even for folk who just happened to live nearby. Some were *designed* to catch fish; others did so while serving some purpose such as milling.

For centuries men fought over the ownership, maintenance and operation of salmon traps (once known as 'hutches' or 'hatches'). Religious communities were deeply involved and sometimes the Abbots themselves would lead their supporters into battle. Fortunately mayhem would usually be followed by calmer periods while the protagonists licked their wounds and waited for the next round. Some used these breathing spaces to go to law over their differences and now and then that worked. In his *Tavistock Abbey*, Finberg (1969) gives a fascinating and detailed account of salmon disputes on the lower Tamar and Tavy, an area particularly prone to such unrest. (Finberg's work is a must for students of the subject.)

One famous incident took place in 1291 when men from the Cistercian abbey at Buckland, near Plymouth, went to a wood for timber to repair their fishing weir on the Tavy. They started cutting at a place owned by the Benedictine abbey at Tavistock, whose forester came across them and was wounded in the arm by an arrow in the ensuing fight. He took the monks to court for stealing timber, but the jury decided the Abbot of Buckland had the right to cut wood for the weir and his accuser was jailed for making a false claim. It seems strange that religious communities would fight over wood, but fish were vital to their way of life and salmon traps had to be kept in good order. Trapping was serious business!

I have been lucky enough to see a hand-written copy, made in 1880, by William Mason, then Superintendent of the Tamar and Plym

Board, of a description of the Buckland salmon trap. Although attributed by him to the Rev. Thomas Moore (1829) it appeared to be closely based on an account by William Marshall (1970) describing the structure as it was when he saw it in 1796. It had a strong timber dam, eight to twelve feet high, 'thrown across the river' between two projecting rocks. At one end was a wooden trap, twelve to fifteen feet square, covered with planks. It had a wide entrance 'contracting inwardly' making it easy for fish to enter. A grate prevented them from passing on through and, as is the way with salmon, few if any tried to go back the way they had come. The trapped fish could then easily be removed by turning off the flow and leaving them high and dry. Marshall noted a key design feature:

It should be observed that the entrance of the trap is placed above the floor so that before the salmon are seriously alarmed by the fall of the water, it as [sic] sunk below the entrance, and their retreat is effectually cut off.

Marshall astutely observed how 'the principal part' of the produce of the fishery was taken by netting the seven or eight pools (some of them very deep) in the mile of river below the weir. Twice a day, four men would drag a seine net through the pools, using horses to carry the net and any fish caught. Where the river was too deep to be forded, trained dogs were on hand to swim across it with their ropes. Given its location low down the river and the barrier of the weir above it, this must have been very productive salmon netting – hardly surprising that Marshall could record:

...after a flood... ten or twelve are frequently taken at a draught... upwards of a hundred, it is said, were once drawn to shore...

Mason had been at Buckland Abbey to record, from an old account book, details of all salmon caught in the fishery in 1792. The catch was down as 1810 salmon, the first taken on 20 March and the last on 18 October with a peak in July. The price per pound started at a shilling and had dropped to tuppence before the fence days (close season – river 'in defence') when the trap was 'thrown open and the fish suffered to go up to spawn'. To the Tamar and Plym Board, in the 1880s, such records would have been from 'the old days' as fascinating to them as they are to us today. Mason would have jumped at the chance to see and copy some of them.

Dom Stephan in his *History of Buckfast Abbey* (1970) describes violent salmon disputes on the Dart between the Cistercian monks at Buckfast and the Dean and Chapter of Exeter over fisheries at Staverton. A deed dated 1228, preserved in Exeter Cathedral's Library, records an agreement between the parties that would delight a modern planner, being in effect a sort of preservation order. The gist of it was that the Dean and Chapter were to keep their fishing weirs without alteration. If they were forced – say, by a flood – to repair or replace them, they had to be restored as they had been before. They had also to maintain an aperture of six feet in the middle of the river (never to be closed by nets, or in other ways) to allow salmon free access upstream. Many years later, tenants of the Dean and Chapter built six new weirs, not to the liking of Robert Simons, the then Abbot of Buckfast, described with understatement by Dom Stephan as a man 'of energetic disposition'. With the assistance of local inhabitants, the Abbot raided Staverton where they broke down weirs, cut up nets, felled trees, assaulted servants and did damage for all of which they were in due course fined £10.

These Dart salmon rows highlight the crucial importance to some religious communities of a steady supply of fresh fish. They are also a reminder that salmon are migratory and when they come in from the sea, those who fish in the lower reaches have first crack at them. This is a distinct advantage over those who fish further upstream and a formula for jealousy and grief that has seldom failed.

Cornish included his own eye-witness observations of ancient traps in his book. One on the Teign had a line of stakes at its foot which guided salmon into a trap. At another, on the Avon, he saw a neat arrangement for catching fish coming down. A mill leat was taking most of the flow at a weir and with it no doubt the majority of descending fish. Just short of the mill, a fender could be lifted diverting water and fish down a steep chute, through a wicker basket and back to the river. All the miller had to do was replace the fender and recover any fish left in the basket. Cornish was assured there were others of that type in operation up and down the river.

He was enraged at Totnes Weir on the Dart in 1821 to discover 'millions of salmon roe' strewn on the banks below that impassable barrier. Unable to reach spawning gravels, the fish were obliged to shed their eggs anywhere they could. They were doomed anyway for the river there was tidal. He wrote:

> ...*the pea lay so thick... a man could not put his foot on the sand without crushing a hundred at a time.*

He recalled a hutch built at Totnes around 1740 by Sir Edward Seymour, so effective it nearly killed off the Dart salmon fishery until the river had scoured for itself a new channel around the obstruction. At its prime this trap so affected the supply of salmon locally that its price rose tenfold. Cornish knew an old man of ninety who had sold a salmon for enough to enable him to buy a cow and a calf, a 'wondrous state of affairs'. He was annoyed because, despite the obvious detrimental effect of Seymour's Hutch, local opinion was attributing the scarcity of salmon to the growing use of lime on land in the area. He pointed out that trout were doing fine in the same waters as salmon were declining, but people would not listen.

The Salmon Commissioners heard much evidence against millers and the damage they were doing to salmon stocks was widely condemned at their hearings. It was said millers should be content with milling and not be allowed to prejudice the salmon. It should be unlawful for a miller to use his mill to catch salmon. Just as they had power to enter a public house, whether a publican liked it or not, police should have powers to enter a mill at any time and search for traps. So it went on. In fairness, not all millers were so inclined. One admitted that in almost every mill there were hutches to catch fish going up and nets to catch them coming down. But he would not allow the hutch at his mill to be used because it distracted his men who would stay up all night and be unfit for work the next day. It was better business to mill than fish.

There was anger that there was nothing to require a fish-pass at mills. They could and often did completely block a river except presumably during floods. A mill weir on the Axe was said to be fourteen feet high, denying salmon access to thirty miles of spawning gravels. The miller in that case reputedly regarded it as his right to kill fish whenever he chose to do so.

Of great concern was the catching of smolts on their seaward migration – a common practice at nearly every mill. Sometimes a net would be used but more often special baskets or boxes would be placed in a mill's leat to sieve-out the descending smolts with wattle or furze put on the weirs to guide the fish to their doom. One witness had seen faggots on a weir preventing what he called 'a living mass of salmon fry' from moving off downstream.

Trapped smolts were boiled and either fed to pigs or spread as manure on gardens. Many were taken by angling, apparently being fatally attracted to red or brown trout flies. Skilled individuals could easily catch a hundred or more in a day. Asked the fate of such fish, one witness replied: 'A poor man would sell them but a gentleman would eat them' which says something about class priorities of the day, but I am not sure what.

Migrating smolts were killed by the cart load, witnesses venturing their own estimates in contemporary measures such as 'two peck-buckets a night' or a 'hogshead-full a day'. Five mills on the Taw were said to be averaging a bushel a night each. A Tamar bailiff told me his father remembered smolts being taken out in 'basketfuls' at Latchley Weir and just thrown on the grass. By any measure, it was a lot of fish and a major cause of the salmon's decline. Some were very concerned. A Captain in the Royal Artillery, who rented a fishery on the Taw, said he had once seen thousands of smolts coming down a tributary and been alarmed to see a turnpike man drawing people's attention to the spectacle. He had told the man it was dangerous to do so and 'given him a trifle' to keep an eye open and see nobody took them.

On the Camel and Fowey in Cornwall, there had long been public antagonism to the erection and operation of weirs preventing the free passage upstream of incoming salmon. In the early 1800s this led to direct action in which fishing weirs in the lower reaches of both rivers were destroyed on the same night. This well-planned event must have involved many strong men and considerable know-how, for these were granite structures with some boulders of around two tons. Not one culprit was detected or informed-upon to the authorities. Motivation for this action was simply that the traps were taking salmon that the raiders wanted to fish for with torches, nets and spears.

There was another incident involving a fishing weir on the Camel that used not only to catch a great number of salmon but also delay shoals of them in the pools below it. This must have been thought vulnerable for at one time a company of soldiers was sent to guard it. That it had needed military protection was confirmed some time later when a great mob broke it up and set it alight. That time however some of the culprits were caught, prosecuted and made to restore what they had destroyed.

In 1860 the Salmon Commissioners heard evidence in both Bideford and Barnstaple about the sad state of the Taw and Torridge. At both sessions there was much said against traps and their operators, particularly about the activities of a Mr John Bastard whom I always think of as 'Trapper John'.

Giving evidence at Bideford, he explained he had been appointed a Conservator of the Taw and Torridge at Quarter Sessions nine years previously. He rented the first hutch on the river (the Bideford hearing concentrated on the Torridge) at the place called Beam. He said the weir was not a complete barrier and every winter fish went miles above it. He described the hutch and claimed it would only catch fish coming up. He fished it by closing the sluices which 'let the water off the fish' so he could go in and knock them on the head. He observed no weekly close time but claimed not to like fishing on Sundays anyway.

He admitted also fishing another trap at a nearby mill where he had taken back fish and sold them for a few pence a pound at Barnstaple and Exeter markets. He was a dealer too and had sent salmon to Billingsgate in London, a great many ending up in Paris.

He described at least a dozen weirs on the river that caught smolts and back fish as well as incoming salmon. Many were 'browse weirs' built of brushwood, laid thick ends upstream, bound together with wattles, then covered feet-thick with clay, stones and rubbish. Branches projected over the downstream pool to make it difficult for fish to approach the obstruction. One impassable obstacle had sharp hooks hung to catch fish jumping at it. Although he was a Conservator, he had never felt inclined to do anything about such things, believing that during the season people had a right to take salmon any way they liked.

The exchanges recorded in the transcript of proceedings suggest the Commissioners were unhappy with what they were hearing. The Chairman (who must have been tipped off) asked if there was any other impediment besides all these weirs. Bastard replied that at Beam there had been a large ridge of stones put there by a previous tenant to stop salmon getting over the weir, directing them instead into the trap. He assured the Chairman that floods had washed this ridge away and he did not intend to repair it ever again. There was evidence to the contrary later that day.

Next witness was a netsman who described himself as the oldest fisherman in Appledore. Times, he said, were hard for the poor local people with fewer and fewer salmon to be caught. It was all the fault of Mr Bastard and the hutches up river. The destruction of smolts made him most angry – 'If you kill all the children, you cannot have men and women'. He admitted not knowing it to be unlawful to catch salmon after 20 October but argued why should he not when Mr Bastard 'knocks them on the head any way he can'.

Then came an extraordinary exchange in which the Chairman asked the witness if he would object to contributing towards paying a few men to watch Mr Bastard. The old man replied that he would not for 'he ought to be caught at it'. Just to be sure, the Chairman repeated his idea of 'a little fund being got up to watch Mr Bastard'. Again the veteran fisherman agreed. So here was a public proposal by the Chairman of a Royal Commission no less, that a Conservator should himself be watched. There was more to come when another netsman said they did not bother to fish for salmon dropping back from Beam because Bastard would have had them all.

Next witness was an angler mandated by a recent public meeting to testify to the dire state of the Torridge. He said the stones at Bastard's hutch, far from being 'washed away', were piled across the river, leading salmon into the trap which had held eight fresh fish one recent morning. Salmon avoiding the stones were likely taken by a man with a gaff – none other than George Bastard, the uncle of John, who paid him half-a-crown a day for his labours.

George took the stand. He was seventy-two and admitted being the first to put the stones in place. The Chairman said now he had reached 'a steady time of life', did he not agree he had done great injury to the river? Not George. He had operated the hutch not for the good of the salmon but for 'his pocket' – an admirably honest reply. The river's decline, he said, was due to the loss of smolts down a local canal – a true fisherman, blaming any hand but his own.

The Commissioners had a weekend off before considering the Taw. When they resumed, an angler claimed hundreds of back fish were being taken at weirs. The Chairman asked if by any chance he knew a Mr Bastard. He certainly did and believed a person who owned hutches should not also be a Conservator. The Chairman asked:

> *Do you think it possible – I do not apply it personally to Mr Bastard – that a person so circumstanced might require one or two people to watch himself?*

The witness not only thought so but told the gathering that the renter of Umberleigh Weir (on the Taw) had as many as eighty salmon in his willey (that part from which water flows) awaiting opening day. The renter was a certain Mr J. D. Bastard, but before he gave evidence they heard from the trap's proprietor who denied it was harmful as salmon were still plentiful locally. Although a magistrate, he condoned catching back fish. The Chairman, who had ridden out to see it, declared he had 'candidly never seen such a malicious trap – it takes everything'. Pressed as to whether Acts of Parliament were to be obeyed or not, the owner tried to justify catching back fish by saying there was a market for them and anyway a good many laws were ignored. This casual attitude to the law was common. At an earlier hearing, the operator of a trap at Weir Head on the Tamar told how one Sunday, when salmon should have had free passage, his foreman had *rather than lose them* 'hooked-out forty' as they were going up.

Bastard returned to the witness chair. The Chairman had seen salmon trying in vain to get over Umberleigh that morning. It being the close season, the trap should have been open, but it was closed and fish could not pass it. Bastard said it had been thus for seventy years and anyway he was only the tenant. He deflected further questions until all three Commissioners gave up on him. They then heard from a Mr Hackwell (H) one of the men who worked the hutch for Mr Bastard. When questioned by Commissioner Ffennell

(F) he demonstrated firm loyalty to his employer, the following exchange being typical:

F   Do you get any fish that are not good?

H   We get some when they come into the hutch.

F   Do you let out the bad ones?

H   No, we have never been in the habit of letting them out.

F   Did you ever let go a fish in your life when once you had hold of him?

H   I did not, and if I had been servant to you I'd have done the same...

He was followed by Mrs Mary Snooks, a fish dealer in Barnstaple market since she was nine. She did not deal in back fish because it was no good for food and she took pride in only selling what she would eat herself. However she knew a woman in the market who took a lot of them. She explained that back fish had white flesh so, to make them saleable, hot salmon blood would be rubbed into them and they would be sold as 'new salmon' for two shillings a pound. With that little trick of the trade testing their appetites the Commissioners concluded their mission and left for home.

Umberleigh Weir, a popular subject at their Taw hearing, had been the cause of much legal activity and violence since the thirteenth century. It was essentially a dispute over salmon fishing rights and at times the action was pretty gruesome, if not downright sinister. One night in 1527, after furious sword fights and attempted murder, men killed three deer then set their severed heads on railings outside the bedroom window of the widow who was then one of the parties contesting control at the weir. Whether this Mafia-style act intimidated the lady I do not know not but it must have disturbed her slumbers for a night or two.

The Salmon Commissioners' report triggered the phasing out of traps and tighter control on what was permissible at weirs. The first big step was that only those structures in use during the 1861 season were given 'privileged' status and allowed to continue fishing. By the 1960s, there were only fifteen of these so-called 'privileged fixed engines' left in Devon and by the end of the Boards' era far fewer than that. One – a large, V-shaped, timber fence – survived on the shore at Lynmouth; another was on a weir down the Avon and that was about that for those ancient fishing devices.

There were however still more than enough troublesome weirs obstructing the movement of salmon. A few were complete barriers while others were only passable in the right water conditions. Fish-passes had been provided at many, some just a notch in the crest of the weir, concentrating low flows alongside a baulk of timber on the face of the structure. These simple and effective passes were common as was the familiar arrangement of pools to give salmon a 'ladder' over an obstacle.

Leats were carrying away large volumes of water from the weirs, to be returned (after use) anything from a few yards to several miles downstream. In low flows therefore, a river might completely dry-up between the take-off point of an abstraction and its return, with dire consequences for its fish and wildlife. An angry angler once tried to draw attention to the effects of leats by having press photographs taken of himself relaxing in a deck-chair, apparently enjoying a picnic in a leafy glade, but actually sitting on the dry bed of the Tavy below a notorious leat abstraction in Tavistock. His point was well made but few people cared and nothing much changed.

One case where the water was not returned was the Tavistock Canal, long a problem for the Tamar and Plym Board and its successors. Built originally to carry copper ores and other cargoes between the mining area of Tavistock, on the Tavy, and the port of Morwellham, on the Tamar, this cut eventually attracted the attention of engineers with an eye for its power potential. In 1932 the Board had to consider proposals for generating electricity at a new works to be built at Morwellham. They were concerned about a proposed residual flow of two hundred cubic feet per minute to be left going down the fish-pass at the Canal's take-off point at Abbey Weir in Tavistock. Finding it hard to visualise, they decided members would need to observe various flows at that point during the summer before making up their minds. Months later, their observations made, they had talks with the developer who kindly offered to do works at the weir so that in low flows there would be more water going down the pass than hitherto. With a cheque for £100 towards reconstruction of the pass, the deal was done. The immediate aftermath was fine. Fish seemed to like the new arrangements so much that the Board, well pleased with themselves, sent a letter of thanks to the developer. Within a decade the relationship was strained, the Clerk reporting that engineers were 'continually producing schemes that would be detrimental to the fishery'. Trouble had begun.

Not far from Tavistock was Latchley Weir, built in the Victorian era to supply water from the Tamar to the Devon Great Consols (DGC) copper mine and in its day a source of great controversy. It was said to be virtually impassable and to have ruined the salmon fisheries. However, a shareholder in the company blamed the increased steamer traffic in the estuary, there being six vessels a day in summer plus another thirty a month for DGC, exporting ore and importing coal. All that activity, he claimed, had deterred the fish; but then, perhaps he had an interest.

A few years later, DGC provided a fish-pass in the weir and by 1869 the Tamar and Plym Board were reporting more salmon in the Tamar. Latchley however still needed improvement and £15 was set aside for that. A year later, press reports said the works had been successful. Bearing in mind their financial position, all concerned must have been delighted when the job came in at £13 – well under its estimate. In 1900 the Duke of Bedford financed a new pass, built to Ministry design, but he went one better in 1929 by having the weir demolished with explosives, allegedly to prevent it being used for power generation.

Smolts and kelts moving seaward were often drawn into leats, sometimes passing through them unharmed and even being helped on their way by judicious operation of sluices. That action was so important that the Devon Board included in its 1959 annual report a message of thanks to mill owners for helping to get the smolts safely to sea. However in some notorious places they were regularly seriously injured or killed by turbine blades. More than once I have found chopped-up smolts in the tail-race of such machines while their operator insisted that no such thing could happen at *his* station.

It was impossible to keep all migrating fish out of leats with mechanical or electrical screens because they soon became blocked by leaves and trash coming down with the fish. Screens needed regular clearing and even the best were not fish-tight, a point demonstrated when a leat on a salmon river was closed for maintenance. On such days an air of carnival would prevail along the channel as the water drained away leaving fish stranded in pools with the old tyres, broken bottles and so on, at the mercy of dogs, gulls, small boys with buckets and larger boys with an eye for the main chance. These events always seemed to fall on sunny bank holiday weekends, to suit leat owners. Guardians of the salmon had to be at such events from about dawn (always referred to as *sparrowfart*) and stay until the fat lady had sung and gone home. On the other hand it was a chance to socialise with colleagues seldom seen and maybe swap yarns over a pint or two.

As well as these hazards for fish coming downstream, there was also a danger that shoals of incoming salmon would be attracted by tail-race water at a mill or power station and it was not unusual when rivers were low to see large numbers of them congregating at such places. While doing so, they were vulnerable to the whims of unscrupulous operators who had ways of poaching with little risk of detection, let alone prosecution. A retired paper-mill hand told me that when he and his mates fancied salmon (as they regularly did) they would simply put size into their tail-race to de-oxygenate the water and kill what fish they wanted.

Salmon in those locations (or just gathered at obstructions) offered such targets to poachers that it was at times necessary to remove temptation by mounting rescues and releasing the trapped fish somewhere upstream, out of harm's way. These were usually big operations involving several men with equipment for catching, holding and transporting up to a hundred or so salmon. Such missions were always a last resort however because of likely damage and stress caused to the fish by netting them out. Even the most experienced bailiffs found it almost impossible to capture a salmon (especially one fresh-run) without it thrashing about and losing protective scales and slime. It must also be admitted that trying to catch salmon in deep pools, *without harming them*, would not have been attempted but for the certainty that others would be along who cared not a jot for the well-being of trapped salmon.

A variation on this rescue theme was tried by the Dart Board in the early 1900s. Worried about the effect on the river of Totnes Weir and a net fishery operating there, they agreed with the fishery's owners to buy netted salmon and put them over the weir, an average of £5 a week to be spent for six weeks, buying at three pence a pound under market price.

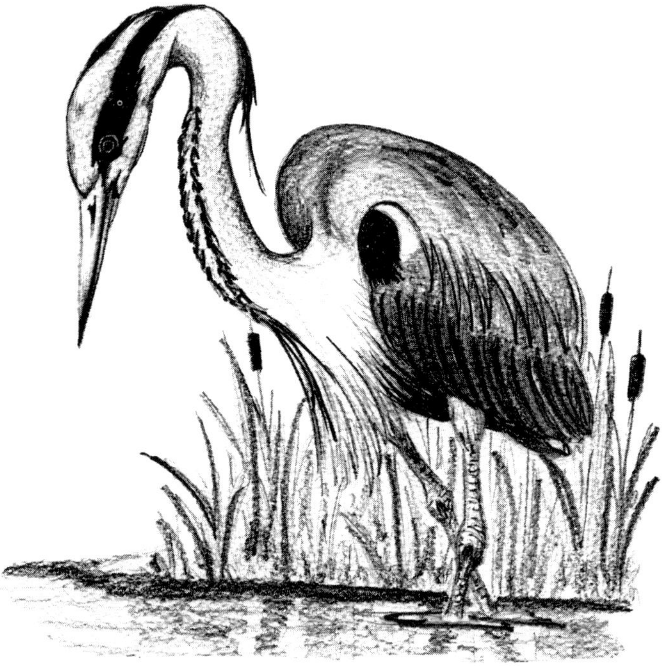

6
Bailiff Force

The practice of employing bailiffs to protect salmon, no matter where they swam, began in the 1860s after the Salmon Commission toured England and Wales looking into the dreadful state of the salmon fisheries.

At their public hearings, one witness after another testified that the salmon laws were being flagrantly violated. Poaching was rife. Most people who lived by rivers were at it. Names, haunts and methods were known, but hardly anyone dared interfere for fear of dreadful reprisals, the villains being numerous and ruthless. Mob rule was but a step away. Large gangs, fifty or sixty strong, with blackened faces, armed with salmon spears, gathered after dark on river banks at spawning time. By torchlight, they would progress, taking fish as they went, daring anyone to stop them. 'Burning the water', as it was termed, was widely practised and dangerous to deal with.

In Exeter a solicitor gave an example of what was going on, claiming that Exe estuary netsmen were daily using nets with mesh below the legal size limit. Asked why they were not prosecuted, he explained it was dangerous for a person to inform on them for he would get 'a body of men upon his shoulders who are not at all particular' – dated language, with a crystal clear meaning. His solution was to have the coastguard care for the salmon in the coastal waters and estuaries, with rural police forces taking over when the fish were in the rivers.

There was however concern that relying more on the police would lead to a surge in other crime: divert them to chasing poachers and poultry would soon be disappearing from the farmyards. As ever, there were not enough constables. One landowner claimed his parish had but one – 'a glorious fellow, but he could only do so much'. Another witness told the hearing how poachers disposed of their fish: they got rid of them, he explained, 'on the sly to private parties'. Indeed they did.

Evidence was given that poached salmon were sold openly on Dartmoor, some cheeky soul having offered one to the Governor of the Prison. It also emerged that the owners of fishing weirs on the Dart were ignoring a law which said they should be left open (not fishing) on Sundays to allow salmon free passage. The Salmon Commissioners were most displeased that such persons 'in a high sphere of society' were flouting the salmon law and setting such a bad example to the poor, lower classes who were so often derided as poachers.

Something had to be done to restore law and order. The expression, 'What is everybody's business, is nobody's business' was heard time and again. The prevailing view was that 'watchers' were needed – 'functionaries', appointed by Act of Parliament and paid out of public funds. By that means they would be respected and have no interest in salmon other than protecting them for the common good. The police and the military would support them as required (and they would *certainly* be required). So came to be appointed the first public bailiffs – official, front line, guardians of the salmon.

From the outset, they have been employed by Boards that were strapped for cash, their main income being from the sale of fishing licences – a fickle prospect indeed, much influenced by events. Thus did the annual meeting of the Tamar and Plym Board in 1902 hear that their income was down because the war in South Africa had taken from the Plymouth area many officers who had for years bought licences for fishing. In 1940 an immediate loss of income of £200, following the outbreak of war, was covered first by borrowing from the bank and then by a Ministry grant of £300 to enable the Board to employ its full complement of four bailiffs. Before that they had been hoping that two of their men would be called up so they could be replaced by cheaper temporaries.

From this income Boards paid the salary of a part-time Clerk and spent most of the rest on their bailiffs. Some were lucky enough to have rich patrons like the Duke of Bedford who regularly dipped into his copper mining fortune to assist the Tamar and Plym Board, which looked after rivers in which he had an interest, in more ways than one. Thus did their Cash Account sheet for 1867 show an income of just over £139, of which £50 was a donation from His Grace. On the other side, the sheet includes expenditure by the Clerk of £1 for 'horse hire' and expenses incurred attending Roborough Sessions to prosecute poachers.

Financially, things were always tight for the Boards. In 1887, for example, one had income from salmon licence sales of £98 and yet spent £101 on bailiffs. Fortunately they had modest reserves to cover this overspend. Not surprisingly they all kept a wary eye on their balances. It was common practice for a member of each Board to act as its treasurer and he would expect at Board meetings to produce his pass book for inspection. The most trifling item was a financial strain as when in 1922 the Clerk of the Axe Board wanted to buy a book on fishery laws and was asked to let it 'remain over for the present'.

For decades bailiffs' wages hovered around £1 a week, gradually creeping to £3 by the end of the Second World War. During both that and the previous conflict the Boards topped up (by several shillings a week) the pay of their men who were serving in the forces. They also paid a 'war bonus' to those who had not been called up, presumably as a reward for guarding an important food resource. Until well into the 1960s, wage levels were tied to those of farm workers, a convenient way for Boards to keep pay matters at arm's length. Casuals were also hired at about five shillings a night to support the regulars as required.

Once war had broken out, the Boards were as generous to their men as they could afford to be but in the build-up they were less charitable. In 1909 a colonel based at Launceston asked the Tamar and Plym Board to allow one of their bailiffs to join the local unit of the Territorial Army. Being of a military disposition they readily agreed provided the bailiff would pay the wages of anyone hired to cover for him while he was away on TA camp. They meant it too, because when he later tried to persuade them to make up the TA camp money to his normal wage, they refused and he was left short.

Special bonuses were not unknown. In 1879, the Tamar and Plym Board voted £1 to each of its five men for services rendered. They did this annually for ten years then replaced it with a more generous shilling-a-week pay rise. They did something most unusual when they passed, to the bailiff concerned, half of a substantial fine imposed on a poacher. Particularly helpful policemen could also expect the occasional tip (usually £1) subject to their Chief Constable allowing it. Officially, this practice died away long ago but many a bobby has since enjoyed a nice piece of salmon or brace of sea trout via his back door. Police assistance could not however be taken for granted. In the early 1900s, the Chief Constable of Devon refused to allow his officers to get involved because if they were injured while acting under a bailiff's warrant they would not be entitled to a police pension or compensation. In 1886 the Tamar and Plym Board had a little trouble clarifying their relationship with the police, their situation being complicated by them having parts of both Cornwall *and* Devon in their area. The Chief Constable of the former had promised in writing to help them prevent infringements of the salmon laws, but the latter would not reply to their letters. They asked their Chairman to contact the Chairman of the Police Committee and bring to his notice the courteous response from Cornwall, a move that would have annoyed the Chief Constable of Devon but one that had the desired effect. Selected sergeants and constables were issued with warrants and Board minutes for some years thereafter referred warmly to police assistance across their area.

Doubts were often expressed by members as to whether bailiffs were earning their wages, especially when their pay was under review. In 1924 the Tamar and Plym Board, having just raised a man's weekly wage by four shillings, instructed their Clerk to make sure he was 'a full-time man' and not spending too much time tending his smallholding. Since he had fifteen acres, that was not unreasonable. The Clerk duly interviewed the man and reported that the land was looked after by his wife and children. Not convinced, the Board made the pay rise subject to the Clerk making 'personal enquiries' that the man was putting in his time.

That case highlighted a perennial problem for bailiffs. Many fishermen seeing one digging his garden or strolling with his wife would jump to the conclusion he was neglecting his river. Word would be dropped to a Board member that the man seemed to have a keen interest in fruit and vegetables or was lucky to be able to spend so much time with his charming lady. Only those of generous disposition would pause to consider he might be working nights, had been out until the early hours and would be on patrol again by dusk. Most Board members believed a bailiff should *always* be on his river, and be grateful for the privilege.

In fact, moonlighting was common and either much frowned-upon or tolerated according to which Board it was and who was involved in what. In my early years with the Devon Board, it was strictly against the rules, on pain of dismissal. That was why I found myself crouched in a Torquay crematorium keeping watch on funerals for a bailiff alleged to be pall-bearing when his time-sheets said otherwise. My companion, an ex-CID inspector from Lancashire, turned Head Bailiff, called this 'a bit of bobbying' and it was well beneath him. He explained how he would have resolved the matter had it been left to him. This involved 'having a word' while simultaneously tapping the side of one's nose with the fore-finger, a remedy that must have reached our man, for he never showed up.

It was difficult for bailiffs to do other jobs undetected, there always being the risk of bumping into someone who knew them. This happened to one man who, in porter's uniform, went tripping down the steps of a country hotel to greet arriving guests, only to find himself confronting the Chairman of the Board and his wife. Never lost for words, he just hissed 'undercover', an explanation he had previously offered when taking money off me disguised as a car park attendant. Truly a man of many parts.

In 1919, in the aftermath of the Great War, a touching incident illustrated the management style of the times. A bailiff (call him Smith) applied to the Teign Board for a pay rise at the end of January. When his request came before the next meeting, they granted and back-dated it from the first of that month. Smith was two shillings a week better off. However, the next item on their agenda was a letter from another bailiff (call him Jones) still in the Army but about to be demobbed and wondering if he could return to their employ. Of course he could they decided – in fact he could have Smith's job if he cared to take it. As it happened Jones subsequently had to decline the offer because the war had left him with both feet affected by a ghastly condition known as 'trench foot'. They gave poor Smith notice anyway, perhaps to ponder on the wisdom of asking for more money.

War veterans were sometimes afforded great respect as when there were two candidates for a bailiff's job with the Axe Board. At interview the first said he did not wish to stand in the way of the other whom he had learned was an ex-serviceman. After that selfless gesture the latter was appointed at £1 per week. He also earned a Christmas bonus of three guineas later in the year for 'he had performed his duties well'.

Bailiffs' jobs were most insecure and entirely governed by finance. If income fell, wages were cut or men laid off until the books improved and that would have been what the men expected. There is no evidence this was ever done as anything but a last resort. Bailiffs were also used to being appointed for a fixed term. William Mason, the Superintendent of the Tamar and Plym Board, for instance was first taken on in 1877 for twelve months with an annual salary, subject to a month's notice. At their Annual Meeting in 1887 he asked for and received a refund of just over £7 for travelling and other expenses. Later that same meeting he was given notice that his services would no longer be required. Although it looked suspiciously like it, there is no reason to think he was fired for claiming travelling expenses.

Boards kept a keen eye on what the others were paying their bailiffs and adjusted their rates accordingly. In 1923 one conducted a wages survey, decided they were being generous and reduced theirs by two shillings a week. I have found no evidence of a Clerk's salary being cut or even subjected to formal survey.

Financial uncertainties haunted bailiffs' lives. In 1919 one man had his weekly wage raised to an apparently handsome £2. However, out of that he also had to rent a horse so in effect it was inclusive of travelling expenses. Even so it suited him fine for ten years until suddenly, in dire financial straits, the Board cut him back to a four-day week to save money. The Clerk reported him agreeable to the new terms, which he had had little option but to accept. Ten years on he began to suffer from lumbago and tendered his resignation. He was thanked for his past services and asked if he would mind continuing for a month to show a replacement the ropes. That was fine by him but war then broke out and the Board, suffering a crippling drop in licence income, were soon £100 overdrawn. There could be no question of taking on a new full-time man. Their lumbago-afflicted bailiff, despite having just resigned, therefore agreed to stay on but accepted that as an economy he would be laid off between Christmas and the end of March each year. When not being paid, he offered to retain his warrant and keep an eye out for some characters known to be poaching salmon with dynamite. Happily this loyal servant was back to full-time within a year, his lumbago presumably behind him [sic].

For many years there was no recognised financial provision for anyone leaving the service although retirement gratuities were common. In 1907 the Dart Board, for instance, voted £50 to a bailiff aged seventy who was leaving after forty years' service. Popular bailiffs were often also rewarded by the members of their local fishing clubs and this gentleman of the Dart, at a special meeting of the Dart Angling Association, received from them an illuminated address (engrossed on parchment) noting his years of faithful service and signed by the subscribers of a purse of twenty sovereigns.

In 1938 the first pensions for bailiffs of the Taw and Torridge Board were such a novel idea they rated press headlines. Their Clerk said the scheme would cost them £22 a year, bailiffs contributing the same sum per week as the Board. He gave examples, unkindly referring to the Superintendent as their 'most ancient employee', a description gleefully reported in the paper and one the poor old chap would have to live with every day.

The consequences of falling seriously ill could be swift and harsh. In 1931 the Fowey Board held a special meeting at which their bailiff produced a doctor's note confirming that he was suffering from pulmonary tuberculosis. They immediately gave him a week's notice on the grounds of ill health, a gratuity of one pound ten shillings and made arrangements to replace him as soon as possible. Members no doubt sympathised with the unfortunate fellow but the written record alone suggests there was little room for sentiment that day.

Others were better treated. In 1920 a much respected Superintendent of the Tamar and Plym Board resigned when rheumatism made him unable to stand night watching. The Board heaped praise upon him, gave him a testimonial 'under their seal' and a wallet stuffed with collected folding money. His replacement, a former petty officer in the Royal Navy, lasted just under eighteen months. Despite his rheumatism, the retired Super returned and of course found poaching to be 'very rife'. When eventually the death of this faithful servant was reported to a meeting of the Board, they stood as a mark of respect. They then agreed to send ten shillings and their deepest sympathy to his widow in acknowledgment of her husband's long and faithful service.

A colleague of his who had for many years looked after the Tamar estuary was most gently eased out. Finally accepting that because of his age, he could no longer cope the Board gave him a generous six months' notice. On his eventual departure, they sent him a letter expressing their appreciation of his work and confirming an honorarium for him of five shillings a week for twelve months.

They had long had a policy of culling older bailiffs on grounds of age alone. In 1880 they openly fired a man just so they could appoint someone younger. Another chap departed the following year, having reached an unacceptable fifty-four. They decided his replacement had to be under forty and they would start him at seventeen shillings a week. The next item on the Board's agenda was a proposal to pay an honorarium to the Clerk for 'extra services' during the year. Whatever they were, it is unlikely his advancing years came into question.

That same Board also had a colourful bailiff who covered the upper reaches of the Tamar. One day he managed to be injured by 'colliding with a motor car'. He was well regarded by the Board and they paid his wages in full while he was recovering. One night ten years later he was attacked by four poachers, one armed with a salmon spear. If assistance had not arrived he would likely have been murdered. Only a few months later, he was fined £1 for drinking after hours in a Launceston pub and the Clerk had to reprimand him severely. However when the incident came before the Board, he reminded members of the man's 'great sagacity and courage' in dealing with gangs of poachers at night on the river. They expressed a hope that in future he would avoid public houses, but wisely took no further action.

Drink had been a recurring problem for that Board but they dealt with it sympathetically. So when in 1894 they fired one of their men for drunkenness, they gave him a few months to find another job which was unusually gentle treatment for those times.

Bailiffs left the service for reasons other than retirement, illness or death. Joining the armed forces for instance was always well received by Boards, flush as they were with ex-military gentlemen of the officer classes. So, when one of their men enlisted, the Dart Board eagerly wrote to his Commanding Officer to say what a good fellow he was. Others departed less honourably. One was sacked for selling poached salmon in Princetown – for a bailiff, a terrible way to go. Another went when it was learned he had been taken to the Workhouse Infirmary in Tavistock after 'drinking heavily and loafing about for several days'.

They were however a hardy lot. Legend has it that one survived repeated falls from the ancient motor bike used for visits to his local pub. On the route home there was a steep, hairpin bend with a scattering of loose gravel on which he would invariably skid. Usually he controlled it but now and again he would slide gently off into the dust. If it was a reasonable night, he was inclined to sleep it off on the verge. Traffic was sparse in those days and he might share the nocturnal wilderness with a few grazing ponies and a sheep or two. Had he passed that way, the local bobby would just have noted seeing the bailiff on night patrol. Those were indeed the days.

There was no automatic leave allowance. Bailiffs had to apply stating 'due cause' for any absence from their duties. In 1931 the full Fowey Board deliberated on an application from one of their men for two days 'holiday' to move to a new house. Even to be away for a few hours could land a man in trouble. In 1895 the Camel Board had complaints that their bailiff had been off shooting for two days. Challenged, he said he had been potting rabbits at the invitation of a friend and had not neglected the river. The Board nevertheless appointed two of their number to 'exercise supervision' over him – despite it having just been reported that, with police help, he had nabbed three of a gang of poachers taking salmon from the Camel.

The job of a bailiff only worked well in an atmosphere of mutual trust. Even with a head bailiff over him, a bailiff would most days decide where he should go and what he should do, with the system relying on his time sheets to say where he had been and what he had actually done. Especially in the early days, there was little close supervision. As on the Camel, members themselves were sometimes deputed to the task by their Boards. Some had their bailiffs keep a full diary and produce it to the chosen member for inspection as required. Such systems worked well enough and were not seriously exploited – wayward individuals being 'leaned-on' by the others who liked the freedom of the job and did not want it spoiled. Nevertheless, the time-sheets of a few individuals were very creative, and a real joy to read.

Accommodation was always a problem. Some Boards paid lodging allowances, others rented or bought cottages to sub-let to their men. Idyllically located by rivers though some of them were, they were hardly a perk of the job. In 1913 the Dart Board had a place for £10 a year in wildest Dartmoor. So close to the water was it that their bailiff claimed it too wet to live in. A committee was deputed to inspect it and they agreed it was a danger to health. The landlord however grumbled that he had already spent £20 on it and did not see his way to spending more. There was nothing else for it but to appoint another committee to look for a better cottage or find a place on which to build one.

Buying or replacing protective clothing was also a matter requiring Board attention. In 1902 the Dart Board passed a resolution authorising the purchase of new waders for a bailiff but only if the Clerk was satisfied the old ones were worn out. Clerks to Boards were usually local solicitors who attended meetings, handled correspondence and dealt generally with their affairs. They were in effect part-time chief executives and invariably prominent members of local society with a certain dignity to maintain. The daily life of this Clerk to the Dart Board would have been filled with matters of law, finance and local politics – far removed from the task of inspecting a bailiff's battered boots – but they were clients and he had their instructions.

Boots, oilskins and other wet-weather gear were issued free, but always with a proviso as to how long they were supposed to last. There was an underlying assumption that the men were getting away with something. Maybe they were digging their gardens or walking their dogs in Board boots and raincoats – thereby wearing them out *unofficially*. There was trouble in store for anyone suspected of doing so. Some Boards had uniforms and the 1884 report book of the Superintendent of the Tamar and Plym Board contains receipts for clothing that make clear the deal for its issue. Two of his men had signed for uniform coats and vests of velveteen, corduroy breeches and leather leggings and undertaken to return the same if they left the Board's employ. They certainly knew where they stood and what they were standing in.

Difficulties arose during the Second World War when clothing could be obtained only with special coupons. This led to such *Dad's Army* situations as the Clerk of the Fowey Board being required by war regulations to write to the Ministry – safely dispersed from London in the Hotel Majestic, Lytham St Anne's – about the pressing need for a pair of rubber boots and an oilskin coat for his man to wear on patrol. Four coupons for the former, nine for the latter and an official 'permit to buy' were duly issued but only after the Clerk had proved to this distant desk-wallah the need for a bailiff to ride his cycle in all weathers.

Purchases of even apparently minor items such as nets and lamps required Board approval. Acquisition of more expensive equipment was usually delegated to committees, some with power to act, others required to make recommendations. Delegating powers to spend money involved a degree of risk, as when a committee of the Dart Board, charged with acquiring binoculars, went off and bought a telescope. Such items were major purchases that had to be carefully guarded. It was understandable therefore that in 1885 the Tamar and Plym Board, having decided to buy a 'binocular telescope', instructed their Clerk to have the Board's name engraved upon it and recorded the decision in their minutes.

The issue of truncheons to bailiffs was once commonplace but the practice eventually died out. Left without these handy weapons, bailiffs claimed they were having difficulty finding their way on night patrols and asked to be issued with larger torches which just happened to be hefty enough to provide some comfort.

One measure that might have helped would have been to allow dogs to be with them on official duties. Officially, bailiffs were not allowed to do so but they would frequently be accompanied by 'strays' they seemed to know quite well. The unpopular 'no dogs' ruling had its origins in placating land owners and farmers when bailiffs first started to go on their land. They were given assurances that bailiffs would not take dogs with them and this became one official line that survived attempts to reverse it.

In 1939, keeping pace with advancing technology, the Boards began to have their bailiffs 'connected to the telephone exchange'. There being no direct dialling in those days, placing a call was a matter of asking the operator for the required number which she (usually) would dial and then put the caller through or say the number was engaged or there was no answer. While not actually listening in, some operators could have learned a bit about salmon but there were probably more interesting things on which to eavesdrop. A typical arrangement was for Boards to pay installation and rental, leaving their men to cough-up for all outgoing calls. This could not last and Boards were soon paying for all official calls.

Telegrams were also widely used. These were usually short messages, telegraphed between post offices, for delivery by boys on heavy, red push-bikes. Not at all suited for emergency response, the system was nevertheless handy for fixing meetings and suchlike. It was also used for transmitting bad news, especially during the war, when the sight of an approaching telegraph-boy was understandably cause for panic.

The earliest bailiffs patrolled mainly on foot, their areas described in such terms as 'from Greystone Bridge, as far upstream as he can traverse'. The more fortunate rode horses, their Boards paying allowances for rental and feed. They would also have cadged lifts on any farm-carts, traps and the like going their way.

Push-bikes then gradually came into favour and by 1910 the Dart Board was paying one of its men £2 a year to use his own machine on duty. Two others received £5 each to buy new bikes and £1 a year to maintain them. The Taw and Torridge Board meanwhile had granted their bailiffs £1 a quarter to use their own machines on official business. However, their Superintendent said that push-bikes had severe limitations in an area the size of theirs. The Lyn was twenty miles away and the upper reaches of the main rivers even further. The train was available but if a bailiff went by rail, it was known as soon as he left the station that 'he is about'. Noting the Superintendent had spent over £20 in fares the previous year and taking his cycle allowance into account, they decided to buy him a motor-bike. They formed a sub-committee, gave it power to act and six weeks later he had his machine. Board meetings were soon regaled with tales of trips to distant waters where poaching was rife and only dealt with by motorised patrols. There was no turning back and before long they were buying a replacement machine for £63.

The Dart Board were also acquiring their first motorcycle which had to have a studded rear tyre, because of the state of Dartmoor's roads. Once the novelty had worn off, it is hard to imagine the bailiffs squabbling over whose turn it was to ride it. Although they were used to horse and push-bike saddles, a few hours on that contraption would have tested the toughest of them. On the otherwise silent moor, it must have been possible to hear from a mile away the noise of the machine's engine and the groans of its rider.

The eventual passing of the push-bike was welcomed by one veteran who told me about the day he came off, at speed. He and a colleague had been out all night. Free-wheeling down a long, winding hill, they were pleased to be nearing home as dawn was breaking. Approaching a farm at speed, they could just make out a few hens pecking at the roadside when through an open gate ambled a huge, muddy pig with very little road sense. The bailiff's cuts and bruises took a while to mend and his bike needed attention. The farmer said his porker seemed to be unhurt but he did spend a lot of time just staring up the hill.

The old push-bikes were replaced by motorcycles which in turn gave way to four wheels. Most of the men would have lobbied members to go for cars as the superior vehicle for the job but the Boards seemed unsure what to do. In 1936 the Tamar and Plym Board resolved to buy a motor-bike, then spent three months failing to find one at an acceptable price. Next they tried to hire a car but could not find a garage prepared to take the risk. There was nothing for it but to appoint a committee and buy one – a Morris 8 saloon. They must have thought it would never end when later faced with a £20 bill from a local garage for teaching a bailiff to drive the new car.

A few old-timers remained loyal to two wheels. One rode his official, green BSA Bantam through to retirement, the steady machine suiting his gentle pace. Up and down his valley he would drone in flat cap, thigh boots and long flapping coat. He was everyone's friend and a good listener. Pausing here and there for a chat, he might hear fish had come up on the last spate or lights had been seen by the river. Normally tight-fisted lads might be buying rounds for a change – with 'readies' too. There could be strangers around and vehicle numbers noted. His was intelligence-gathering the old way, slow but sure. Courtesy was nearly his downfall. When riding his machine, it was his habit to hang on tight, speedily executing unavoidable hand-signals. Approaching friends he would throw a quick salute, wobble about a bit, regain control and be on his way. He never actually crashed, just raised the area's blood pressure. It is said that once, in his local pub, just for a laugh, someone claimed he was after a bigger bike and, before the penny dropped, a hush had descended like mist on a sunny day.

Relationships between Boards and their men were often strained. A recurring grumble was the way the bailiffs treated anglers – insufficient deference shown, chaps not knowing their place, that sort of thing. In 1935 the Tamar and Plym Board solemnly discussed complaints about the way bailiffs were asking to see licences. They were apparently getting well into a good natter about how the fish were taking and so on before revealing their identity. Not fair play thought their Board; bailiffs, they ruled, before commencing conversation, must *always* introduce themselves and show their warrants. This was (still is) the sort of thing committees decide that alienates the men in the field. The intention was obvious but the instruction to bring it about needed to be followed with discretion. Applied literally, it would have infuriated regular fishermen who would have called it 'Bureaucracy, gone mad'.

Tips were a source of trouble. Bailiffs were public servants, not ghillies for the gentlemen they met. However, should they perform a service – land a fish perhaps or suggest a fly – then some small reward might be offered and the question was: how could that be refused without giving offence? The Dart Board decided to clarify the position by making it what they called a 'penal offence' for its bailiffs to accept money. They even had printed on their licences a notice to fishermen not to 'offer gratuities' just as a zoo might ask its visitors not to feed the monkeys. However, when a fisherman used bad language to a bailiff, they obtained a written apology: they could not, they asserted, 'allow their servant to be abused and sworn at in the exercise of his duty' – almost as bad as offering him a tip.

Bailiffs had ways of getting their own back on anglers who treated them badly. One was to wait until they came upon them casting a line where the noise of the river made it impossible for an approach to be heard. A sharp tap on the shoulder with a shouted 'Good morning, sir' usually produced a gratifying reaction, with a chance of the victim taking an early bath. If that happened, it was well known that few bailiffs could swim.

For all Boards, there was always a lingering – sometimes justifiable – suspicion that some of their bailiffs were in cahoots with the poachers. In 1885 the Taw and Torridge Board formed a sub-committee to find and engage three trustworthy, honest men as watchers on the estuary where poaching was rife. The police were stuck with the job because the bailiffs were in with the poachers and they were keen to pass it back to the Board where it belonged. Even in those harsh times it proved hard to find a trio willing to face the hostility of their community for such employment.

Mistrust prevailed in 1922 on the Dart. On rivers like the Dart it was customary during the peak salmon spawning weeks to pack the bailiffs off to lodgings in the upper reaches near the fish. Most of the men hated this duty which kept them far away from home and resented by communities in which they were just temporary intruders. Moreover, they were themselves closely watched, hardly able to leave their digs without it being known 'they were about'.

The Dart Board were convinced that all was not well on Dartmoor, so a committee was deputed to investigate. They went without their bailiffs so the locals might speak freely and they heard plenty. They reported 'from evidence that could not be gain-said' that as many salmon were being snatched off the spawning beds as were caught legally. The bailiffs were given a stern warning – they must spend all their time on the Moor watching the rivers. They were not to lodge together and one was to stay in Princetown where poached salmon were freely on sale. If they were 'active', said the Board, they should have no difficulty securing convictions – in fact, their jobs depended upon it.

Besides chasing poachers, bailiffs did other work such as cutting bankside vegetation, raking spawning gravels, repairing banks and bridges and removing and burying diseased fish. Now and then they also had the unpleasant task of recovering dead horses and other farm animals from the water. These they usually cremated by the river in fires of wood and straw.

There was never any shortage of aspirants to the job, with hundreds applying for a vacancy arising. A preference for appointing retired policemen and ex-servicemen gave the service discipline and experience of life but left it short of breath in pursuit of younger villains. All the bailiffs were men, the job then being thought unsuitable for a woman. There was little union interest or membership. A new bailiff starting could expect no formal training but one of the old hands might be asked to show him round and 'put him in the way of matters'.

In the South West there has been less violence used against bailiffs than in other parts of the British Isles and mercifully few have been seriously injured. However, abuse, threats and scuffles have been commonplace and bailiffs have also now and again had getaway cars driven at them. One man, warding off a salmon spear, had it driven clean through his hand. Others have been menaced or attacked with oars and knives. Their families have been intimidated. A bailiff living in an isolated spot had men shouting and firing shotguns around his house when his wife was there alone. Another had paint daubed all over the front of his house and poured through his letter box. Vehicles' tyres have been slashed and radio aerials twisted or snapped off. The guardians of the salmon have had much mental and physical aggression to contend with.

Few assaults by poachers resulted in court appearances with sentences severe enough to satisfy the bailiffs who were convinced that magistrates valued salmon above bailiffs. That view came from cases such as the one when a veteran bailiff was seizing a gaff from a violent poacher who managed to crack him hard over the head with it. For poaching, the miscreant was fined £8, for the assault only £1. Boards believed fines imposed for assaulting a bailiff were ridiculously low and many of them should have been jail sentences anyway. They were sure such leniency tended to encourage violence and periodically they tried to do something about it. Letters of protest would be fired-off to the Lord Chancellor's Office, the local Clerk of the Peace, MPs, the National Association of Fishery Boards and anyone else who might be able to bring influence to bear. It was *always* a waste of time and effort. Replies were invariably negative; Justices had absolute discretion, their independence was sacred and the Board should have known better than to write in such a fashion. Members were usually left muttering and exchanging thoughts about who knew who in the right circles and when they might bump into them... quite by chance, of course.

Relationships between bailiffs and poachers have ranged from mutual respect – the sending of Christmas cards has been known – to deep, mutual hatred. There have however been lighter moments as occurred early one morning when a bailiff made a startling discovery. He was patrolling an area in which salmon would congregate at a weir where poaching by the locals was a way of life passed from one generation to the next. He walked the small river, alert for signs of activity and at the weir he could see someone had indeed been active. On the concrete had been painted, in white letters, two feet high, the legend 'BOLLOCKS TO BAILIFFS' – a heartfelt expression of local feelings. As soon as they could, the men proudly gathered by it for souvenir photographs.

Another memorable incident took place on the Taw and Torridge estuary when bailiffs found they could not approach to observe some men netting at night without their presence being signalled by the frantic barking of dogs left in a strategically parked car. There was no other route than past the guard dogs. Something had to be done, so the following night the bailiffs came prepared. Creeping up to the car, the hounds within again going berserk, they passed through the cracked-open window, several bars of laxative chocolate... then withdrew to a safe distance to await developments of a potentially explosive nature.

There were private bailiffs too, working for fishing clubs and the like, sharing the same risks as those publicly employed. Indeed, one tragically lost his life in what was thought to be the line of duty in the little Devon town of Tiverton on Saturday 30 July 1887.

Early that morning, the body of Mr Archibald Reed was discovered in the Exe at a place called Collipriest. A bailiff with the Tiverton Fishing Association, he had been working alone for some time against a gang of local poachers who had been taking advantage of the river being low after prolonged dry weather. The previous night he had received information that four men would be netting some of the town pools and after supper had gone out after them telling his wife not to expect him back before breakfast.

He was found dead shortly before six by George Davey, a gamekeeper who had also been on night patrol. Walking by the Exe, he saw a body in the water by the opposite bank. He hurried on towards the town and sent a lad he met to call the police. Constables Raymond and Sparkes, with Davey's help, then removed the body from the water and trundled it home on a hand cart, there also to break the terrible news to Mrs Reed.

Reed had worked for the fishing association for only one season. A stonemason by trade, he had for some years been in the King's Own Regiment from which he was invalided-out. He was thirty-seven, of fine physique, broad build, medium height and genial countenance; not a man to be dismayed by heavy odds, he was greatly esteemed and trusted. Said the press:

> *He knew he was dealing with a class of fellows more or less reckless of spilling blood and with hazy ideas of right and wrong.*

At the crime scene there were signs that there had been a desperate struggle. His stick, broken, splintered and stained with blood, was there suggesting he had cracked someone hard with it. Beneath an elm tree in a meadow bordering the river was a pool of blood, a trail from which reached to the water. By the pool were found a pocket knife, a clay pipe, a wooden pipe and a handkerchief. Nearby was also a piece of rope, such as was used for tying sheep's feet. The finding of his pencil and pocket-book on the deceased was taken to indicate he had intended to take the names of the poachers when he had caught them. Of these articles however it was the hanky that caused the most excitement, for it was not his. It had blue and white squares and had evidently been tied in a knot and used as a neckerchief indicating, it was believed, that its wearer was a man from the country. This was thought to be a vital clue to the identity of the murderer whom it was assumed had inadvertently left it behind.

Press reports of the event said it had caused the utmost excitement in Tiverton with police energetically pursuing enquiries. Since poachers were thought to have been responsible, officers were searching for clues – especially blood-stained clothing – at the houses of known operators. A number of likely suspects were detained but released after questioning. One habitual poacher volunteered for a medical examination, causing a great commotion because it was thought he had been arrested. He was a suspect because Reed had had him convicted more than once. However he had previously had both arms broken and was judged incapable of having committed the deed.

Rumours were rife and the public so excited that, said one reporter: 'trifles light as air become confirmations strong as Holy Writ'. An old tramp washing his feet in a water chute, became a man cleaning blood off his clothes. Men in a nearby village seen covered in blood were found to have been killing sheep. Two strangers turned out to be furniture removers on their way to work. A suspect seen covered in dirt early that fateful morning, had been a drunk walking home after missing the last train and 'lying about the place'. A man had cut a length of rope from a halter hanging on a pub wall – was that the length found at the scene? At Sidmouth, the camp of the 3rd Devon Volunteers was shaken by rumours that a detective was there after a member of the Tiverton Company. A navvy with a bruised face was said to have been arrested in Cardiff and was being brought to Tiverton by train. This was met by three hundred people but neither prisoner nor escort alighted for the story had been a hoax.

Rumours were fuelled by the state of affairs prevailing in Tiverton. A councillor claimed at a council meeting that in the town there were well-known characters who never did a day's work but always had plenty of money and were continually loafing about the streets. The Mayor tried to stop the outburst as being a matter for the police but the councillor exclaimed that they get their living after ten at night and before six the following morning by poaching and in other ways. A farmer said Tiverton was 'a roost for poachers and rogues' at which someone pointed out, amid laughter, they did not roost – that was the trouble.

Further details emerged at the packed inquest which began with the coroner leading his jury to view the body. Then, giving evidence, George Davey, the gamekeeper, said he had met Reed at nine on the Friday evening in an inn and offered him a drink. The bailiff had told him poachers were liming the river and he was going after them. They talked over who might be asked to assist but neither could think of anyone they could trust. Davey had said he would be out that night and would help all he could. He had passed by on the other bank at a quarter to four but had neither seen nor heard anything. Returning later he had noticed marks on the grass, seen a body in the water and raised the alarm. Despite his excellent character his testimony 'excited some surprise'. Why, it was asked, had he gone for the police rather than first checking there was nothing he could do for the victim?

Distraught though she was, Mrs Reed gave evidence. Her husband had told her four poachers were going to net a pool that night; a man he knew, his nephew and two others. She had been very worried, asking him what he could do against four. He had said he would wait till they were down at the water then come up behind them and ask what their little game was. She had told him they would murder him but he thought they would more likely run and said, 'If I don't die before I'm murdered, then I'll live to a good old age' – words so ironic they must have stunned the inquest. They had been married three years. He had been a sober man, so conscientious about apprehending poachers that she had long lived in fear of him losing his life. She identified his pocket knife, pipe, blood-soaked scarf, lead pencil and scissors-case. Her confirmation that the blue and white chequered hanky was not his led the local police chief, Superintendent Crabb, to hold it aloft asking all to see and let him have any information they might have as to its owner.

Police had been out on their foot patrols and PC Sparkes described a nocturnal meeting with the bailiff during the night before his death at about two-thirty. He had remarked that Reed was about early. The bailiff had replied there was something doing down the river and he wanted to catch them at it. He had not mentioned names. A PC Symons had also spoken to Reed who had told him poachers were liming the river. The name of Reed's suspect had come up. A workman gave evidence of finding the bailiff's cap on the road leading out of Tiverton. It had been a fine, clear morning. He had also seen two boys, a stone-breaker and a man from the village where he was going. Nothing untoward. Sickening medical evidence was then given by the police surgeon who catalogued the injuries sustained during what must have been a ferocious knife attack. He considered the bailiff's own pocket knife could well have been the murder weapon.

A special meeting of the Tiverton Fishing Association was convened the next day to discuss the murder of its servant. It was well attended, despite the short notice. The chairman read out letters received from members indicating support for offering a reward and helping the poor widow. They openly discussed her circumstances and wondered whether she might get lace mending work at which she was skilled. They voted to pay her ten shillings a week for a month and appointed a small committee to arrange for an appeal. They were cautious about a reward until they had seen what others would offer.

All the Borough Police (Tiverton had its own until 1943) and others from the surrounding district were engaged in the enquiry which was thorough in the extreme given the resources available and the lack of much forensic science capability. When the alarm had been raised, Superintendent Crabb had immediately sent a telegram to the Devon County Constabulary at their barracks in Exeter:

> *Water bailiff murdered on bank of Exe close to town. Murderers unknown: must have blood on clothing. Let County Police know.*

This led to telegrams being dispatched to all County Police stations in Devon and the net began to spread. The Exe was dragged and volunteers from the fishing club combed the woods near the scene but nothing useful was found. Efforts by the Watch Committee to obtain the services of a detective from Bristol or London both failed. Eventually a Detective Inspector Hills, a murder expert, was called in from Plymouth. The Chief Constable of Devon had a personal tour of the crime scene. An early police deduction was that the awful deed had likely occurred between one and two o'clock because all the dogs in the area had howled then and could not be hushed.

Suspicion fell mainly on a thatcher from a nearby village. Repeatedly questioned, he gave the press accounts of all the points put to him and the answers he had given to confirm his innocence. A squad of police visited his cottage, taking possession of a coloured handkerchief, but nothing came of it. In the town there was deepening distress because nobody had been arrested and charged. The Watch Committee offered a reward of £125 for information leading to the conviction of the guilty person or persons and notices were posted throughout the area. The Home Secretary, after great procrastination, eventually offered a free pardon to any accomplice of the murderer who turned informer but with no such amnesty for the one who had committed the crime.

By mid-August Detective Inspector Hills had returned to Plymouth and Tiverton had begun to settle down. There were however still incidents related to the murder. One day a rumour spread that a much respected constable in the neighbouring parish of Burlescombe had been murdered by a gang of poachers and one of his attackers was in custody. Telegrams flew to and fro and there was great concern until, after several hours, his senior officer discovered the supposed victim safe and sound at his post. The story had arisen because of a squad of artillerymen marching through en route to Okehampton. They had exchanged banter with the policeman, ribbing him about a constable who had been murdered near Wolverhampton at a place called Bilston. This had been overheard and, because it sounded just like the local name for Burlescombe, another rumour had taken flight.

There was further excitement when a young man 'of the agricultural class' was brought from Exeter for questioning. Not a suspect, he held a possible lead for the police. He had been in the town two or three days before the murder staying in a well-known lodging-house. There he had overheard a group of men plotting to murder Reed should they encounter him on their nocturnal forays. He had hoped they would be detected without his assistance but could no longer withhold his information, receipt of which stimulated further futile police work.

By early September, still nobody arrested, police must have had mixed feelings when a respected gentleman gave them information, obtained at seances, claiming to have 'witnessed' the murder and to have been given two names. The local paper left its readers to judge but commented that here was a chance for spiritualism to make its mark or go down in history as 'impudent delusion'.

There was yet another false alarm shortly afterwards when a constable discovered a heap of clothes on a dung heap in some allotments. Bearing suspicious traces, they were taken to the station for examination which concluded they had been destined to adorn some gardener's scarecrow when he had got around to it. Murderer's clothes they were not.

Tiverton Quarter Sessions took place towards the end of October. In his opening speech, the Recorder said that, since he had last had the honour of addressing the grand jury, a murder had been committed in the Borough that had become notorious throughout England and until the perpetrators were caught, 'a heavy bloodstain must rest upon Tiverton'. He described the efforts being made in the case and asked for the inhabitants to aid the police bring those guilty to justice, for they were not far away. At the next Sessions three months later, the case had still not been solved and went unmentioned in official speeches.

There was however a development of sorts in Cornwall, roughly two and a half years after the murder. On 19 November 1889, the *Tiverton Gazette* reported an incident that had taken place in Millbrook, a village just over the river from Plymouth. Under a headline 'Sensational Rumours from Cornwall' their reporter told the story in the long-winded style of the day. An 'evening contemporary' had started things off by claiming 'extraordinary revelations' and a 'supposed clue' to the identity of the perpetrators of the unsolved murder. Word had reached Tiverton that a navvy and his wife had been having a row during which she, it was alleged, had shouted at him:

> ...*Thee knowest thee told me thee killed the keeper when we were courting...*

Rumours started immediately that her accusation concerned the Tiverton case and the local police had been called. The Borough force had not heard officially but its Superintendent had sent his men to find out who had left the town during the past twelve months. Exeter police knew nothing more than was in the paper and the reporter concluded that a journey to Plymouth and a boat trip across the Tamar were unavoidable. He told the readers he did not arrive there until gone midnight and presumably then had to wait for the morning ferry.

He gave his readers plenty of local colour, starting on the crossing. Cornwall apparently was more attractive when approached by boat, Millbrook being better from a distance than close-to. On arrival he met PC Davis (*Mr* Davis as he was courteously called in those parts). This 'obliging and communicative officer' escorted him all the way to the village, past several street corners, each occupied by groups of loungers who indulged in 'audible surmises' as to the business the constable had in hand.

The navvy was working on fortification works near Millbrook and had been lodging with his wife and child in an apartment house for the past ten months. Residents and neighbours who had heard the exchanges had told their stories and there were conflicting accounts of what had been said. The navvy's wife was a high-spirited woman with a tongue that was 'not always under command'. The altercations had been 'pitched in a high key' with the lady screaming words to the effect that he was not going to do to her what he had done to the gamekeeper. The lady had cooled off though and was not looking to incriminate her husband. He had allegedly assisted in the murder of a gamekeeper but, if it had happened at all, that was several years before the Tiverton event. PC Davis, made his enquiries, took statements, reported to his sergeant and took no further action. The *Gazette's* reporter summarised:

Despite protracted enquiries, both by the Borough and County Police, nothing was elicited to justify an arrest although popular suspicion was for a time directed against various people.

The Tiverton Museum of Mid Devon Life has a walking stick bearing the carved features of Mr Archibald Reed. They also have two halfpenny coins found on his body and given to them by the grand-daughter of a police inspector involved in the investigation. As far as I know, this case remains unsolved but... perhaps you know better.

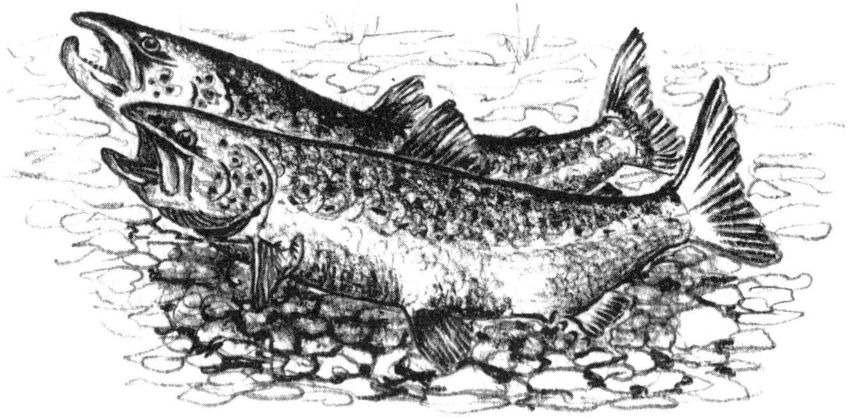

7
Portions of Poached Salmon

The illegal taking of salmon to feed a hungry family is perfectly understandable and having 'one for the pot' is traditional in country areas. Sympathy for people driven to that has over time characterised poachers as noble peasants, persecuted by fishery owners and the forces of law and order. As its heading suggests, this chapter is a collection of poaching tales from the days of the Boards, not an in-depth review of the subject. From countless incidents, only a handful have been chosen to show what the guardians of the salmon were up against. It is for the reader to decide whether salmon poachers should be regarded as petty criminals who specialise in fish, or folk heroes, or even – heaven forbid – 'lovable rogues'.

Salmon poaching was well established in the South West in 1608 according to a story in Edward MacDermot's book, *A History of the Forest of Exmoor.* This relates to disputed fishing rights and is a graphic account by witnesses to a night-time salmon poaching excursion on the Barle, referred to as the 'Barrell' (as pronounced locally). The witness described what appeared to have been a classic burning the water episode with a three-man team: one of whom was on the bank carrying the catch and keeping the fire going with dried reeds, while the other two were in the river, fishing with salmon spears.

Another glimpse of the early poaching scene (1796) was given to us by William Marshall. Referring to the Buckland Fishery on the Tavy, he was not surprised it was poached, being next to a mining parish 'notorious for its pilferers' who came mob-handed 'bidding ten or a dozen men defiance'. They preferred the net by night and by day the spear, which they threw 'with great dexterity'.

Typical spears had a stout wooden handle, four or five feet long, to which was attached a heavy, metal head with barbed tines and were either purpose-built or adapted from forks made for legitimate uses such as shifting dung. As far as I know however there was no British Standard for salmon spears.

Cornish wrote angrily about spearing on the Dart in the early 1800s. He considered it to be a dreadful instrument used by poachers who would have been better employed in an honest calling. Poaching, he argued, encouraged idleness, for men thus engaged at night could hardly be fit for labour by day. He even claimed that young timber was suffering because poachers had taken to carrying the spear heads in their pockets and cutting a fresh sapling handle when a fish was spotted. He knew one family had speared sixty 'old' salmon and carried them into their farmhouse.

The Salmon Commissioners heard many such tales during their tour of the area in 1860. On Sundays in December, for example, there would be twenty or so fellows spearing salmon in the course of three or four miles of the Avon. On the Axe, salmon were taken with lights and spears when they were spawning and after a flood it was common to see people out with spears anywhere along the river. The picture was much the same elsewhere. Around Totnes, foul fish could be bought for three pence a pound – a quarter their normal price – during what should have been the close season. All were taken by spearing, mainly at night with lights. An experienced spearer answered questions for the record when the Commissioners visited Bodmin to hear about the Camel. He came from the river's upper reaches and had always used a spear for fishing. He went out by day and caught the fish in deep pools. If the water was muddy, they would throw in a stone which made the fish 'get into a hover' so they could see them and be able to use their spears. On the spawning beds, hidden in hides made of gorse branches, they would simply watch the hens and kill any cocks that came calling.

The vicar of a parish near Camelford had never known a salmon killed with a rod and line. They were all speared, a practice known as 'salmon hunting'. He had been out to see it done. Some of his servants had taken straw which they lit to give themselves light and attract the salmon. They had killed two fish which were said to have been perfectly edible despite it being December and in a spawning area.

Another clergyman described coming across a group of men acting oddly on the Taw. They had the whitened skull of a horse tied on the end of a rope and were dragging it through the pools to frighten salmon to the banks where they were easily speared. He believed this was a common practice. At night a white-painted board or stone might be positioned in the water so salmon attracted by lights would be easier to see and spear against their light background.

A salmon spear was included in the feudal dues to Prince Charles, Duke of Cornwall, when in 1973 he visited Launceston, the Royal Duchy of Cornwall's ancient capital. With this odd gift – receipt of which caused HRH much amusement – was a strange assortment of offerings including one hundred shillings, a jar of cumin, a pound of pepper, gilt spurs and a brace of greyhounds. While pondering on his great good fortune, HRH would have been interested to know that nearly a hundred years earlier the Superintendent of the Tamar and Plym Board, whose area included Launceston, briefing his members on a Duchy matter, explained that the Cornish word for a barbed spear was a 'barbague' and they were used for 'killing salmons [sic] in the Tamar'. Even so, HRH probably preferred his rod and line.

Pulman, in his *Book of the Axe*, described an extraordinary way of taking fish that he termed 'groping'. He had seen a person, who could not swim, go down ten feet or so in a salmon pool with a swimmer standing on his shoulders to keep him down. An experienced groper, said Pulman, might surface with a fish in each hand and one in his mouth. He did not mention the fate of the inexperienced.

A carpenter had a different approach. One day a miller was leaning on a gate near the Avon, taking a break from grinding corn. Quietly contemplating the price of flour, he heard a gun fired and saw a curl of smoke rising from the river. Investigating, he met a carpenter carrying a nice salmon that he had just shot in the head, a misdeed for which an Exeter court fined him £2 with seventeen shillings costs. That day the magistrates also heard four spearing cases against labourers of the same area who were also each found guilty and fined £2.

In 1894 the Tamar and Plym Board employed an extra man to watch the Plym's spawning beds, thought to be at risk from navvies building the nearby Burrator Dam. Special precautions were also usually taken when railways were under construction since dynamite intended for blasting cuttings had a tendency instead to get lobbed into salmon pools.

Not all loud bangs were poachers at work. Early one morning bailiffs heard that miners were dynamiting pools on the lower Tamar. They discovered that explosives were being used to break up a log-jam in an attempt to find the body of a man who had fallen in and drowned several miles upstream. Although fish had been stunned, they tactfully took no action. Had the miners been poaching, they would likely have met the fate of a man that year convicted of using explosives to destroy fish – a month's hard labour without the option of a fine.

There was concern about the use of lime as a poaching aid, for it was in common use on the fields and readily available to those with a mind to put it in rivers. One Whit Monday, a gang did just that on a minor tributary of the Tamar. They came with wheelbarrow and bucket, three young lads, moving along the stream, methodically throwing lime into every pool. Said an eye-witness: 'They were in the water groping with their trousers turned up to the knee'. They made off with twenty of the best fish, leaving dead ones behind in every pool. As far as I know, this ruthless gang got clean away... but the file is still open.

Snaring fish with a noose of rope or wire was popular as was snatching them with a gaff made by tying a hook to the end of a stick. Worth next to nothing, these tools were easily hidden about the person or discarded at no great loss. Rivers with clear water, where fish could be easily seen, were particularly vulnerable to snaring and snatching. The Plym was one such and many thousands of salmon were removed from it by these methods. A typical incident was reported by a bailiff in 1883. Information had been received that men from a nearby mine had been seen poaching the river, so he concealed himself there. He soon saw two labourers and a blacksmith from the mine walking the banks, looking into pools and obviously searching for fish. Then one went down on his knees, made a thrust at the water with his snatch and quickly had a salmon on the bank. The bailiff swiftly nabbed him and seized the evidence. Would that it had always been so easy.

An opportunist poacher would just make an implement if need arose. A bailiff watching the Torridge early one morning, saw two young men coming towards him along the bank. They noticed something in the river, so one got a stick from the hedge and began to beat the water with it. He then used it to catch and kill a salmon, which he hid in the lining of his coat. When stopped and searched by the bailiff, he admitted being 'caught fair' but later, in court, claimed to have only removed a fish that was already dead. Witnesses then swore on oath the truth of both versions of events but the magistrates found the case proved and the poacher, who had been unemployed for months, was £2 worse off.

Salmon were taken in various ways. One day a bailiff came upon a man attempting to snare them using a horsehair halter with which he boasted of having had much success. He had no more joy with that particular instrument. Continuing his patrol, the bailiff came across two men – one a farmer, the other 'a miller out of trade' – in the river filling a sack with fish caught using an anglers' net. More entries for his notebook. Next day, a country policeman booked three farmers in the same area for using poles to drive salmon into a large net. That same summer, all concerned were on the lookout for a man with a donkey reportedly on his way from the north coast to net the Tamar. There are unfortunately no further records of this mystery man or his possibly holy mission.

In 1884, a bailiff had a holy encounter with two Benedictine monks he found attempting to remove a fresh salmon from the Dart with their bare hands. The Dart Board withdrew a summons against them following representations that their conviction would cause great pain and annoyance to the Community at Buckfast. They were allowed to apologise, pay costs and accept they would never again fish the Dart. Soon afterwards, bailiffs found two men in the same pool driving salmon with a pole towards a large 'net' they had made out of wire netting. Not being monks, they had their day in court.

Those days the police used to know what was going on and were often in the right place to catch poachers wet-handed. So it was in the village of Horrabridge early one morning in 1884. The local bobby was lurking beneath a tree, alert for trouble, when towards him came a young labourer of that parish carrying an implement. 'He was wet and the prong was wet' noted the constable, 'this attracted my attention to him'. A person carrying a salmon then came into view and disappeared into a nearby house. PC Jones made inquiries and discovered that the son of the lady of the house, aged twelve, had caught the salmon with the help of the prong man and his implement. The lad implicated another man who, when Jones went to see him, said, ' I didn't do much to catching of 'un sir, I only caught 'un by the tail once'. With that cleared up, questioning revealed another player in the drama. The boy's older sister had apparently thrown her apron on the salmon when he had tossed it onto the bank; then she had given it to the man first seen carrying it – *enough already!*

It is amusing to consider how much would have been known about what happened in Horrabridge that morning had PC Jones travelled out from Tavistock or been responsible for other villages as well. As it was, even though he had seen only part of the action, he knew the players and ensured that justice was done.

On a Cornish beach, at four in the morning, another policeman was watching the wake of a small boat reflecting the full moon. Smugglers seeking a landing place? Movement on the nearby beach then caught his eye. Where a small stream ran across the sands, a figure was spearing sea trout as they splashed through the shallows. The constable strolled over, invited the man to accompany him to the station and relieved him of the manure fork he was using as a spear. Several fish already in his coat pockets were seized as evidence. On a later date the defendant, described as a beer-shop keeper, told magistrates that he had fancied a walk on the sands and there found the fish among the seaweed. The ever sceptical bench asked him to be good enough to leave £2 with them on his way out or face the consequences.

There were attempts to combat poaching by other means. For instance, rewards were offered for information. In 1890 the Axe Board posted handbills around their district offering £2 for information leading to a conviction of any person illegally taking salmon. This must have been very tempting, but there would have been a fear of awful retribution for 'grassing'. However, one gentleman told the Salmon Commissioners that he had distributed handbills offering rewards of £5 and one poacher had informed on a companion for that. A sneakier way of catching poachers was a clever 'sting' heard about in Cornwall in 1824 when a local paper reported that a man was going around making inquiries about obtaining a salmon spear. Said the item:

Should the unwary produce such an instrument, it is seized and the owner brought before a magistrate and fined for possessing it.

Many had been entrapped by this ruse. For the benefit of the paper's urban readership, the report carried a footnote explaining that salmon poaching was usually carried out at night, by two people, one holding a blazing torch to attract fish and the other a three-pronged spear or trident. Just in case anyone did not know.

The nineteenth century was tough for the poor fishing communities around the estuaries of the Taw and Torridge where the fishermen were regularly locked in fights with bailiffs and police. Causes of this strife were the poverty of the fishing families and their attitude that salmon were sea fish, to be freely taken like any other. The Taw and Torridge Board saw it differently and made the fishermen buy licences and obey regulations governing seasons, methods and so on. These were regarded by netsmen as impositions on behalf of the rich men who fished for sport rather than survival. There was little love lost between the parties.

The Salmon Commissioners heard an outsider's opinion of the situation when the Inspecting Commander of the Coastguard gave evidence before them. A Scot, he had been stationed at Barnstaple for three years. He claimed to be appalled by the wanton destruction of salmon with small-mesh nets and the lack of observance of close seasons. In a fairly obvious bid for departmental growth and greater influence, he had only two men but with more he was sure coastguards and police could at least put a stop to fishing at improper times. One of his men said a great many salmon were taken and dispatched by rail to London. He had seen them in Appledore, packed in baskets, going to 'a certain party' in the city.

A local magistrate suggested that public watchers were needed with power to search packages under a magistrates' warrant. He had had it on 'unexceptionable authority' that ever since the fence days had begun, old soap boxes full of salmon had been sent to London, consigned to a dealer in Billingsgate. As much as seventy or eighty pounds went every night by mail train. The Town Clerk of Barnstaple just happened also to be solicitor to the railway company and knew the identity of the mystery receiver in London. He was sure that some 'active and intelligent officer, whose business it was' could follow up the lead. That was the trouble – there were no such officers.

It is hardly surprising that when bailiffs were first appointed, they met with resentment and violence. A typical incident took place on the Taw in the late summer of 1871. Acting on information received, a bailiff, a constable and a keeper were on the lookout for poachers one Saturday night at a place called Umberleigh Bridge. Just before midnight they saw six men with sacks, later found to contain seventeen salmon. The press reported that these 'fellows' attacked the policeman and bailiffs, beating them with sticks, but they were 'worsted'. Four took flight, leaving behind their spoils and two of their number were arrested and held in cells until the Monday when they were taken to court. The report also tells of an accident that befell the constable driving them to town. For some reason his horse bolted and the poor chap jumped or fell out of the trap and was seriously hurt. His prisoners escaped injury.

Up the two rivers and around their estuary, bailiffs and police were pitting their wits against determined adversaries who believed they had right on their side if not the law. Sometimes the poachers would be caught – more often, they would slip away to net again another day.

One raw November night in 1861, a lone policeman was by the water in the little port of Appledore. Pacing up and down to keep warm, he was under orders to watch for offending fishermen. Now and then cloud obscured what moon there was, but he could see well enough. So could the man with a bag who emerged from a fishing boat, tied up nearby. At the sight of the law he fled, dropping the bag on the quay. The constable went pounding after his man, ordering him to stop and blowing his whistle, but the fellow was clean away. His bag had in it two large salmon which were seized in case he was traced, but he was not.

Policemen in that area were tenacious in their pursuit of fisheries offenders. At one o'clock, one November morning, two constables were on duty at Fremington on the estuary of the Taw. At low tide they observed a boat with four men shooting a net near their vantage point. They immediately launched their own boat to go out and search the suspect crew who pulled away downstream when they saw police approaching. Shouts failed to stop them and a chase ensued. When the unfortunate police ran aground on a shoal, the poachers went ashore on a nearby sandbank and pelted them with stones. One officer was injured before their jeering assailants tired of their sport and made off. Later, in court, they did not even bother to deny their offences and were each fined five shillings plus costs.

The following year, two bailiffs were keeping observation near a place known as 'Old Walls'. Just before dawn they saw two boats acting suspiciously and ordered them to stop. At this, one pulled hard away with the bailiffs' boat in hot pursuit. As they neared the fleeing craft, one of the fugitives swung an oar and caught one of the bailiffs a violent blow on the head. His hard hat absorbed some of its force, but it still knocked him out. His partner recognised their assailant as the coxswain of the local lifeboat and shouted that he had almost killed his colleague. The poacher retorted that if they would pull closer he would finish the job and threatened to shoot them if they tried to stop him fishing again. Ashore, a doctor confirmed a compound fractured skull. It was some months before the victim was fit to give evidence, but when he did the coxswain got four months hard labour, his sentence mitigated by previous good conduct and lifeboat service, during which he had saved many lives.

The salmon wars raged on year after year with scores of cases brought for fishing out of season, using nets with undersized mesh, possessing unseasonable salmon, obstructing a bailiff, assault and so on. Attacks on the bailiffs were commonplace and although sometimes followed by jail sentences, stiff fines and prison terms had little lasting effect.

There were differing points of view about salmon poaching and whether to take it seriously. This was illustrated in 1871 when a vicar became involved in the prosecution of a poor fish lady who had exposed salmon for sale just a few days into the fence months. The local press published several letters, signed with pseudonyms such as 'A Lover of Fair Play' and so on, asking how a clergyman, who should practise peace and goodwill, could have been guilty of such heartless conduct. Others wrote supporting the vicar and the issue boiled away nicely. Eventually, the editor expressed his view that the vicar's action was not altogether creditable in a clergyman and since it was his paper, the matter closed.

Another reflection on prevailing attitudes was a report of a meeting of the Taw and Torridge Board in 1883. Representatives of the netsmen were asking for a reduction in licence duty from the then statutory maximum of £5 to £4. The noble Chairman thought the higher fee justified since the nets caught all the fish. The netsmen said they only fished for a living and a reduction would be a boon. A member, certainly no diplomat, said they would just spend it on drink. Not so, responded the netsmen, they were abstemious and could not afford to drink anyway with catches as they were. The Board rejected the request. Furious and threatening to talk to their MPs, the fishermen claimed that so many fish were going up river they would eat each other's spawn – implying they would be performing a service by removing some. They said there was any amount of poaching going on – a 30lb fish had been seen at the railway station the previous week yet it was nearly Christmas and in the fence days, and a shop in town had poached salmon openly for sale.

A glimpse of contemporary mores appeared in a local paper in December 1887. A case was pending against a man caught carrying a salmon, scarcely concealed in a bag, in broad daylight. It said, although he had not been very clever:

> *Very few – certainly not all the magistrates – regard the offence as particularly heinous. The crime principally consists of getting found out. It is not an unknown experience in Bideford, about this time of year, to be confidentially asked if you would like a nice salmon. But, as a rule, the purchaser does not see anything of the fish until the shades of night have fallen. Then it is delivered in secrecy and with rapidity.*

The paper had a story about a woman who had entered a local shop and sold the tradesman a salmon. Asked when he might have it 'the fair one' calmly informed him she had it with her and 'proceeded to disengage it from the region of her dress improver'. This, thought the paper, was an exceptional case.

Such tales were amusing but romanticised versions of what was happening. Salmon poaching was not funny for those involved. The ugly scenes that took place in 1889 in Barnstaple more accurately reflected the prevailing mood in the area. The incident began during Police Court hearings one January day. Several fishermen of Braunton, an estuary village, were to appear in court for illegally taking salmon, assault on a bailiff. A large crowd of supporters had come with them for the proceedings.

They were first annoyed by a case in which a bailiff, admitting a mistake, withdrew a charge against a fisherman but the magistrates would not allow the accused his expenses. Then came an announcement in the late afternoon that the bench had so much business to deal with they were adjourning the remaining fishing cases for two days. Press reports said this heightened the ill-feeling among the fishermen. One rushed to the front of the courtroom shouting that his children would starve if he had to spend another day going to court. There was uproar, with at least a dozen men climbing onto seats bellowing to be heard. County Police in attendance tried to quieten them but a melee ensued involving fishermen, bailiffs and police. Scuffling spread to the landing where the crowd tried to throw a couple of policemen over the rails.

Women with the fishermen were screaming for them to fight on as a dozen Borough Police arrived and ejected the crowd onto the street. There they hung about, shouting threats and surging forward whenever they saw a chance to storm the building. Fights broke out while the angry mob waited for court to end. When it was finally over, a strong body of Borough Police escorted the County officers to their station and the bailiffs to the railway station, followed all the way by a large, hostile crowd. One injured constable was also a part-time bailiff against whom the mob had a 'special animus'. He had been so badly kicked and scratched he had to be taken home in a cab – no doubt thankful it was not a hearse. No arrests were made at the time but the ringleaders were known and court appearances followed in due course.

The troubles of the Taw and Torridge were not confined to their lower reaches, nor perpetrated solely by the working classes. Far from it. Upstream, many with a happier lot in life regularly enjoyed the sport of fishing for salmon kelts, despite it being unlawful to do so. The Salmon Commissioners were told that every gentleman on the river killed them. A vicar lamented their slaughter, the season past (1859), he had known of two men taking eighty on the fly. He blamed all this fishing for foul fish on the coming of the railways. He excused it by saying that since there was no fly fishing for salmon to be had at any other time, people would fish for back fish rather than not fish at all, legal or not. Clearly, the better-off were quite happy to ignore the law when it suited them.

There was too a wealth of evidence that poachers were taking salmon regardless of condition. In Cornwall, a rule of thumb was to regard as edible any fish not actually working on the spawning beds. A lieutenant in the Royal Navy declared that people who had only seen them in Cornwall did not know what good salmon was. It was not uncommon, he said, for fish to be put on the table, so soft the spoon would fall right through it. Another witness told how gourmands would 'look for the pea', a reference to the eggs, when ready to shed, being about the size of peas.

Whatever the state of the fish, the stimulus for poaching them was undoubtedly the thriving export trade to France. Charles Dickens, referring to salmon caught during the close season and en route for France, quoted witnesses describing the contents of the boxes as 'a mass of putrefying garbage, with spawn oozing through the packages'. The Salmon Commissioners in their Report concluded that 'the ingenuity of French cooking succeeded in making palatable that which in its natural state would have been both distasteful and injurious'. *Bon appetit!*

Further insight into the taking and use of foul fish comes from Webster. In 1889, an old man who lived by the Bovey told him he could remember the river being lit up on winter nights by the torches of men spearing salmon and how ill the foul fish used to make them. But the old man had learned the hard way. When himself a lad, he had been made so sick by salmon which his farmer employer had given to him, that he had never eaten it since.

Webster told a tale of a lone salmon in a Bovey pool one dry summer. Trapped by the low water, it grew uglier and leaner with the passing weeks until a gypsy removed it. Webster was so astonished that anyone could eat such a disgusting thing that, when next he met the local coroner, he asked him if he had sat on any dead gypsies recently. They could not, he felt, have dined on anything worse 'since their forefathers had left the banks of the Ganges on their first fortune-telling and kettle-mending expedition'.

But he had a soft spot for the poor and hungry. One day, reviving a kelt in a stream, he heard a whisper from the bank opposite urging him to take care or it would get away. Taking pity on the man, he gave him the fish which he said was twelve pounds of perfectly wholesome food. The man later told him it had been the 'best hake his missus had ever tasted'. At that time, 'hake' or 'red hake' were common names for kelts which were openly sold as such.

Preserving salmon and keeping them edible was an eternal problem. Apart from salting-down in brine, one way was to hang them up cottage chimneys on special hooks – a tradition called 'kippering'. Many an innocent visitor must have enjoyed hospitality beside a humble hearth while out of sight curing in the smoke of logs or peat, was the catch of the day and the catch of days before that.

Let nobody suppose the transition from nineteenth to twentieth centuries brought an end to our rich poaching traditions, for it did not. Just as they had always done, spears flashed in the moonlight and nets drifted in forbidden waters. However, a variety of modern inventions were applied to the business. Water sports gear proved the greatest boon: wet-suits, flippers, snorkels and face masks were warmly welcomed, as were the inflatable dinghies and spear-guns that went with them. Sometimes modifications were made to such gear. One lethal example was a high-powered, cross-bow adapted for poaching by welding razor-sharp barbs to its bolts. Lightweight, man-made fibre, gill-nets were also a boon to weary poachers, tired of humping heavy hemp about.

It was however the arrival of motors that truly transformed the business. Trucks, vans and cars extended the range of local poachers and eased for them the burden of carting away their catches. With such transport, they could reach distant waters and supply far-away markets. Yet, alongside the modernising, ancient practices were being kept alive.

So it was that in 1928 a poaching quartet came before a crowded Exeter Police Court in a case described by the prosecution as one of the worst for many years. There had been a lot of poaching in the area but efforts to trace the offenders had been unsuccessful. The men were charged with putting lime in a city leat with intent to destroy fish and with taking salmon from the leat. They pleaded guilty to the latter but denied the liming. The wife of one was also summoned for aiding and abetting the offence having bought quantities of chloride of lime from a local chemist's shop on two occasions a month apart. At her third attempt, she was refused the chemical as also was one of the men who had tried later. Even to the unwary, it must have been clear that a big operation was in prospect and the Exe Board would likely have been alerted. But as ever only the poachers knew when and where they would strike.

The leat in question had an intake point well upstream of a mill which it supplied with water power. One Saturday in June, the mill manager had carried out his routine evening inspections and assured himself that the fenders at the intake were in order with the leat carrying some five or six feet of water. At dawn the following morning, a railwayman, on shunting duty at the railway yard some distance downstream, noticed three men paddling up the river in a boat with a fourth walking along the bank beside them. They were heading in the direction of the mill. The shunter thought he recognised two of them. Ten minutes later, a railway signalman saw them going from the river towards the mill.

Nobody saw what happened when they got there but, from the evidence, it was not difficult to work it out. After they had gone, the mill manager discovered his sluice had been shut and his leat drained down. In the remaining foot or so of water, it was easy to see a large number of dead coarse fish and some salmon. Also at the scene was a sack still containing chloride of lime. By the leat, there was blood on some stones where the heads of fish had been hit against them. Clearly, the leat had been lowered, limed and plundered of its best salmon.

Meanwhile, a few hundred yards downstream, a man watched a mooring below his bedroom window, wondering where his boat had gone. He had looked out at dawn as usual and been startled to see it was missing. As he observed the scene, he heard the splash of oars and his beloved craft reappeared, rowed by a burly, unfamiliar figure. He shouted down and asked the rower what was afoot. The ruffian said he had only been across the stream and cleared off without another word.

The following morning, the husband of the lady who had bought the lime had hired a lorry from a contractor for eleven shillings and used it to collect thirty-seven salmon from a cache by the river and transport them to a fishmonger in Exmouth. He had telephoned the receiver from the contractor's office and been heard to say he had forty or fifty 'you know what' to dispose of. After some bargaining, a shilling a pound was agreed and fourteen guineas changed hands for nearly three hundred pounds weight of salmon. On the journey back, words had been exchanged as to how come only thirty-seven salmon had been available for sale when forty-nine had been taken from the river? Someone must have spirited a dozen away, but who had known they were there? Wherever they went, the main batch, consigned by the Exmouth fishmonger to Birmingham, were seized by police at Exeter.

No chances were taken with the court case. An experienced fish merchant gave evidence as to the condition of the fish. Lime, he explained, made their gills fade to white at the edges and their eyes blur. The Chairman of the Exe Board said undoubtedly the fish had been killed by lime but no analyst could prove it. The court heard that lime acted by stripping oxygen from the water thereby suffocating the fish – handy background for poachers following the case.

All four were found guilty, three being jailed for three months, the fourth having the option of a £10 fine or two months inside. The lady was found not guilty of aiding and abetting. Her husband, with several previous convictions for poaching, invited to address the court, said with feeling, 'I wish I was a bank clerk.' During the investigation, the dodgy Exmouth dealer had admitted to buying fish from one of the poachers for twenty years, but *never* salmon. But then, he would say that... wouldn't he.

Lime has not been the only substance put into rivers by poachers, there being other chemicals that can kill or stun fish yet leave them still edible. But using poison to poach salmon was never very smart, if only because of the unavoidable litter of dead fish left behind after the event. The method was therefore never used by those who wished to take salmon regularly yet remain undetected. These professionals were instead perfecting an approach that would eventually account for a great many salmon. Alongside the traditional poacher was coming a new breed, in it for the money and nothing else. The lovable rogues had company!

Rumours that poaching was taking place on a scale previously unheard of began circulating in the early 1960s and were dismissed as exaggerated. Newcomers, it was claimed, were working just a few areas but with great success. They were choosing places where the local bailiff was known to prefer a quiet life to investigating tales of gangs in the night. Some of the poached fish were said to be reaching the legitimate market through – of all places – Budleigh Salterton, a famously staid resort. Such stories of salmon being 'laundered' were ignored and other clues dismissed. One night a Torridge poacher became entangled in his net and drowned. It was confirmed he had been no stranger to the nocturnal Torridge but this was not taken seriously. Those well placed to know were ignored. A much respected netsman swore repeatedly that the best pools in the area were being done but his warnings went unheeded.

Then bailiffs began to find more signs of poaching activity and encounter the perpetrators, a majority of whom were from a small town in Dorset. The 'Bridport Gang', as they became known, were pioneers of a new order and an unwelcome threat to salmon stocks. A loose association of men – some with criminal records unrelated to salmon – they fished the lower and middle reaches of the main salmon rivers, at night, during spring and summer. They would drive into the area in teams of up to four men. Sometimes women would accompany them as cover. Some would wear respectable clothes, a help if stopped. It was their practice to net more than one river each trip, staying in the area overnight to do so. Their usual form was to leave the car well away from a chosen pool to which they would walk carrying nets and dinghy. Nets might be tailor-made for each location, set under the surface and tied to a tree root with a hidden rope. They would be virtually invisible, easily missed by searchers. No light would be shown and precious little noise made. Later, gear and catch would be taken back to the car or an arranged rendezvous. These were common features but what happened during an actual incident would depend on who was involved and prevailing circumstances. There were no rules.

So it was that early one morning two bailiffs came across an empty car parked in a lane near the Taw. Suspicious, they called for police assistance. Two policemen arrived and with the bailiffs settled in for a long wait. Eventually, they saw four men coming towards them across the fields, clearly heavy-laden. The bailiffs broke cover and ordered them to stop. The four took off dumping sacks and gear in bushes as they ran but they were caught and detained. They had obviously had a productive night for on the ground were seventeen salmon and four sea trout. Nets, dinghies and other fishing gear were also found. A most interesting discovery was a road atlas in the car on which were ringed many rivers and pools. Good reconnaissance was a key feature of their operations.

One legendary character could do the job solo. A typical encounter took place one night when bailiffs were watching the Taw. Again, the first sign of trouble was a car pulling into a lay-by not far from the river. Its lights went out and no activity was detected. A driver taking a nap perhaps? After an hour, the bailiffs went to examine the river and found a net in place. Not long afterwards, a man was seen to walk silently across the field. He threw a few big stones into the pool – an old trick to spook fish into the net. They shone their torches to reveal a man in a rubber dinghy retrieving the net and removing fish. Ashore, he refused to identify himself or any companions who might be with him. Suddenly, he gave a sharp whistle, as if signalling to someone, then bolted from his captors, crossed the river and disappeared. The weary bailiffs had no option but to wait until he returned to his car. No other person was seen or heard during the entire incident.

At the Cornwall Board, rumours about the Bridport Gang had been circulating for some time before positive contact was made. The alarm came one June day from the private bailiff who looked after the lower Tamar. The tide had gone out at the most downstream weir to reveal, stretched bank to bank, a gill-net with several salmon in it. We assembled a team, met on site and concluded that an operation had been interrupted and probably abandoned. We searched the area and on a bank overlooking the weir found a den with items of equipment and clothing. Stuffed into a shoe, to cover a hole in its sole, was a sheet of a Bridport newspaper. It was as if a calling card had been left for us and we knew for certain we had trouble on our hands. Predictably, all-night surveillance drew a blank and we were left to contemplate the implications of this new threat.

The outsiders did not long have the pools to themselves. Locals were soon in evidence, using similar methods. Thus did bailiffs and police discover a car hidden by a Tamar pool some three hundred yards off the road. There were paddle handles in the car. A search of the river bank revealed a dinghy with paddle blades to fit the handles from the car. In the river was a gill net. Those eventually charged – one a fisherman from Plymouth – claimed they had gone to the river because the weather was too bad to go to sea. Understandable, but illegal.

That was an interesting case in that police forensic evidence tied the paddles to their handles by matching spots of paint found on both of them. However, forensic work sometimes drew a blank. Tired of being spotted by their number plates, seasoned poachers one day hired a car from a well-known agency. When examined for evidence the next day, this was said to be the cleanest car ever returned to the rental fleet – no trace of anything interesting was found. It had been used then 'wiped' by an expert and returned before the office opened for business.

As well as all this action around the rivers, a traditional activity was developing nicely on the coast – the taking of salmon in nets under cover of fishing for sea fish. Hot spots for this caper were the beautiful rocky coves of Babbacombe Bay in south Devon. Fishermen there had fixed nets marked by buoys and would check them when they lifted their crab pots. Salmon and sea trout from the nets would be hidden away aboard the boat for the return to port. An operation to combat this type of poaching usually started with observations before dawn by a team hidden on the cliffs above a suspect net and pots. They would watch and make notes while the crew of the *Lulu Belle* (or whatever) checked their nets. The team then made a dash for the vessel's home port hoping the salmon would still be aboard when they caught up with her. The first 'walkie-talkie' radios made a great difference to such operations. Cumbersome and temperamental though they were, they made it much easier to track a boat along the coast and have a welcome party waiting in harbour or on the beach when the salmon were brought ashore. Landing them at a beach in summer made life harder for the bailiffs. A gathering crowd of sandy, nosey, cornet-licking kids, with even nosier relatives, was not an ideal audience when poachers were refusing to be searched and turning nasty. The crowd usually sided with the poor, persecuted fishermen and it once took the police to restore order when they saw that a bailiff with his radio had been 'spying' from a nearby deck-chair.

Let it not be thought that anti-poaching operations were invariably successful. Bailiffs and police did not always catch the villains and even the simplest operations went wrong.

They did so one night when a couple of experienced bailiffs spent several soaking hours watching from a nearby hill for poachers on a stream that dawn revealed to be a wet and winding road. Fortunately there had been no traffic. Imagine their reaction had a car appeared along what they thought was a river. Ghost stories have been based on less!

A similar incident is said to have happened one night involving a bailiff whose eyesight was not great but who was well liked and rightly 'carried' now and then by his mates. Because of his local knowledge, his head bailiff assigned him to look after a couple of men from another area who had come in for a joint patrol. It was a delightful night for a walk; they disturbed a pheasant or two, a dog fox crossed their path, owls kept them company and the dawn chorus was at its magnificent best. There had been no sign of lights or poachers – peace had come to the river. This could have been because the trio, wrongly assuming their local pal knew where they were, had actually been wandering around in a wood, unaware that they were out of sight of the pools they were supposed to be watching.

They tell another tale of the short-sighted one that may or may not have been true. Again he was on night patrol with visitors in his care when he became entangled in a very prickly hedge while leading them to a favourite vantage-point in an adjoining field. The strangers, waiting to follow, were trying to shove him up and over from behind when one of them made out a gate just a few yards away that made it possible for them to stroll round and welcome him with open arms when he finally broke free. Too much local knowledge can sometimes be a burden.

Another day a veteran bailiff was crouched in a hollow watching his river. It was November and that time of day they call dimpsey or between-the-lights. Way downstream, he saw a light, bobbing along the bank, coming his way. A poacher for sure. Behind the first there then appeared another and another until finally there were nine lights approaching. A gang out of Plymouth maybe? Whoever they were, he was not about to stand in their way. So he just lay still, pulled his hat over his face and hoped for the best. Only at the very last minute did he peep, see miners' lamps and hear the caving group go clanking by.

Just waiting for poachers could be embarrassing. One bright summer day, a bailiff hid among large granite boulders above a favourite spot on the Dart. It was near a tourist honeypot but people were staying around their cars. He was watching for the local lads, none of whom cared about it being broad daylight. If there was a salmon to be had, they would try for it. Colleagues were nearby, in radio contact. A young couple then appeared, stripped off and dived into the pool. He could hardly show himself without being accused of peeping. So he kept his head down hoping they would soon clear off. Unfortunately, when they emerged, instead of dressing, they compounded his dilemma by – shall we say – physically expressing their emotions on the river bank. All he could do was sit tight, switch off his radio and wait.

An unusual tale concerns one evening when two bailiffs hid beside a popular poaching pool on the Tamar. It was almost dark when a courting couple came sauntering along the path. In those days, bailiffs' torches had a tiny, battery-level warning bulb which they used to mask with tape. On this occasion, one light was bright enough to show through the tape. Unaware of this, the bailiffs just sat tight expecting to go unnoticed. However, as the couple drew level, the lady spotted the light in the bushes and thought it was a glow-worm. Unfortunately, she bent down to get a closer look. Experienced though they were, this was too much for the pair in the bush and one of them chuckled. Even in Cornwall, glow-worms do not often chuckle, so the lady's hysteria was understandable. There must also have been some explaining to do as to why two men were hiding in bushes beside a lovers' lane.

Sometimes, the good guys just got lucky. At four one morning, a policeman was at a filling station near Exeter when two men, trousers wet to the knees, paid for their petrol with wet £5 notes. Stopping them as they drove away, the police found they were carrying wet nets, dinghy and sacks but no fish. The nets, said the poachers, had only been in the sea and had caught nothing. However, tiny organisms taken off the nets were shown only to live in freshwater and both nets and sacks were plastered in salmon scales. The catch had already been sold and delivered. In court, it was said in their defence that on the night in question they had caught nothing but a bad cold.

Another lucky night, police in Exeter, speeding to a burglary, saw a man running down a road near the Exe. They caught up with him lying across the front seat of his parked car in which he had tools for housebreaking as well as the usual poaching gear. To save on his overheads, he even had with him a tube and can for siphoning petrol, but it was luck he ran out of that night, not fuel.

When apprehended, poachers have offered outlandish excuses. Once, following the discovery of a suspicious parked car, bailiffs and police, with tracker-dog, found two men lying soaking wet in a nearby field. Asked to explain, they claimed to have been listening for a nightingale. Naturally, as dedicated students of bird-song, they knew nothing about the poaching gear and salmon the dog was sniffing-out just a few yards away.

Poachers have long been attracted to nightingales. Early one morning, the grass wet with dew, a man in a wet-suit was found lying beside a spear-gun and bag of salmon. He too explained his passion for the song of this magnetic bird and desire to stay dry while waiting to hear it. In the dark, pure chance had led him to lie beside the incriminating articles. Maybe poachers had left them there, he suggested, anxious to assist the forces of law and order.

Reasonable people might think the mere wearing of a wet-suit could, in certain circumstances, be difficult to explain. Not a bit of it. For example, a suspected poacher, taken to a police station, was found there to have on a wet-suit under his jeans and jersey. Cynical officers thought this a mite suspicious but he explained that it was worn to help his varicose veins. Doctor's orders, of course.

Circumstances can be so misleading. Bailiffs once came across a man, waist-deep, in a river, holding a gaff – in effect, a hook on a stick usually used for catching salmon. On the face of it, he might have been thought to be doing just that. However, what had happened apparently was that, the previous day, he'd been trying out a new surf board at that very spot when he'd dropped his St Christopher charm. So he was looking for it, using the gaff to search the gravel. Fancy being accused of salmon poaching – the very thought.

One lady poacher had an original excuse. She was, she explained, pregnant and had been overcome by a craving for fresh salmon. More plausible than a man fined for having a salmon in his house who said his little lad had picked it up in the street, thinking it to be a herring.

Poachers feared certain courts with good reason. Some young lads who lived by the Avon once took drastic action to avoid appearing before their local bench. It happened that the bailiff knew there were three big salmon in a pool near their village. It being a weekend, he was keeping a special eye on them. The river was low and the fish could clearly be seen. Irresistible, for certain lads of his acquaintance. On the Saturday evening, before retiring, he noticed a boy cycling up and down past his house. From his bedroom, he saw the lad stop and glance up. When he took off his waistcoat, as if going to bed, the observer jumped on his bike and peddled furiously away. Mounting his own machine, he went as fast as he could to the salmon pool, arriving just in time to catch the three lads with one of the precious fish. He took their names and let them go. However, when he went to their homes on the Monday to interview them, he found they had taken the train to Devonport and joined the Royal Navy.

This bailiff had better luck when he became suspicious of a man limping towards him from the river. He stopped the fellow who was clearly ill-at-ease and anxious to be on his way. As they exchanged a few words, a salmon slid slowly out of his trouser leg and onto the grass at his feet – a difficult thing to explain away.

A husband-and-wife team used a similar routine. He would snatch a fish, then tie it with cord around the ample waist, beneath her coat. They would then rely on bailiffs being reluctant to stop and search the slimy temptress, for fear of sexual allegations – however improbable they might have seemed.

Poachers were not always too bright in court, especially those who watched over much American courtroom drama on TV and thought they knew the form. I once saw such a pair before magistrates in Ashburton. They had been charged with using a snatch to take a salmon from the Dart and their defence was they were miles away at the date and time of the alleged offence – it was nothing to do with them! For the prosecution, a public-spirited witness gave evidence that he had seen the accused kneeling on a rock in the river, shouted to attract their attention and taken their photograph when they looked round. Copies were available. Being an English court, I am not sure it helped the defendants for one of them to leap to his feet shouting *Objection*! With his solicitor and the Chairman of the Bench trying to stop him, he said the photo' wasn't them, it must be someone else – he *had* heard the shout (confirming his presence at the scene) but was *much* too smart to let the witness take his picture. It slowly dawned that maybe he had blown it for them both.

Hiding and moving the catch has always been a challenge to poachers. In estuaries or along the coast they might simply pass salmon to another boat to bring ashore. Sometimes they would tie them in a sack to a buoy or sink them with a weight for collection at low tide. Ashore, they might move them about hidden under sea fish in boxes. For sheer cheek however it would be hard to beat the lady apprehended in 1927 wheeling a large (35lb) salmon along a street in a perambulator, pausing now and then to let friends admire 'pretty baby' in the shawl.

Dodges and inspired excuses were not the monopoly of the working class. Those using rod and line were not above seeing what they could get away with. They could be quite reticent when it came to paying for a licence to fish. Sometimes offenders were so high and mighty there were fierce disputes as to whether or not they should be prosecuted. At some time, all Boards were faced with what to do about 'distinguished persons' caught fishing without a licence. A typical case was in 1908 when there was close voting by the Dart Board before one of their bailiffs was instructed to proceed against a 'General Sir X' for this offence.

The Tamar and Plym Board had to deal with something similar at a meeting just before the start of the Second World War. Their Clerk had begun legal proceedings against a brigadier, said to have killed a salmon in an illegal manner. Addressing the Board, the Clerk hoped little would be said because the brigadier had died. A captain, supported by a colonel, said the case should not have been brought against this distinguished soldier and man of such high social position, without Board approval. Non-military members however supported their Clerk's impartial approach.

Boards did not prosecute all offenders. A bailiff one day found a fellow fishing the Dart without a licence apparently believing it to be the Tavy for which he had one. They let him off. But another unlicensed character, in 1941, thought he had a unique excuse. He had sent five shillings for a licence during the Plymouth blitz. It must, he said, have been destroyed in the flames for he had not received one. They did not let him off. A cheeky vicar said he had not used his licence so could he have a refund? The Clerk sympathised but he could not.

If he had been a serviceman, he would not have needed a licence because members of His Majesty's Forces were allowed to fish without one, a freedom enjoyed by many on leave or in transit. In wartime, to increase the nation's food supply, there were also relaxations of the fishing laws governing such things as the keeping of kelts or using gaffs to land fish caught by rod and line.

An abiding memory of those times is of a bored army, awaiting embarkation for the invasion of mainland Europe, given to lobbing grenades into salmon pools to enliven their camp menus. According to legend, American GIs were leading exponents of this logical fishing method that ignored all that business with rods and licences. In 1944, the Clerk to the Tamar and Plym Board reported a little poaching by our allies, but nothing too serious. Very diplomatic of him, with D-Day in the offing.

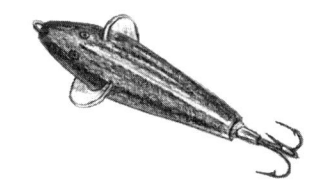

REFERENCES

Anon. Report of the Commissioners Appointed to Inquire into Salmon Fisheries (England and Wales) together with the Minutes of Evidence HMSO London 1861

Ayton, Warwick. *Salmon Fisheries of England and Wales*, Atlantic Salmon Trust 1998

Bielby, G.H. 'An Attempt to Establish Rainbow Trout in Cornish Streams 1968-69', Cornwall River Authority Report, 1971

Chope, R. Pearse. (ed.). *Early Tours in Devon and Cornwall*, David & Charles 1967

Clark, E.A.G. *The Ports of the Exe Estuary 1660–1860*, The University of Exeter 1960

Cornish, J. A *View of the Present State of the Salmon and Channel Fisheries*, 1824

Dickens, Charles. *All the Year Round*, Weekly Journal 1861

Dickinson, M.G. (ed.). *A Living From the Sea*, Devon Books 1987

Finberg, H.P.R. *Tavistock Abbey*, David & Charles 1969

Finberg, H.P.R. *West-Country Historical Studies*, Augustus M. Kelley 1969

Fort, R.S. & Brayshaw, J.D. *Fishery Management*, Faber & Faber 1961

Grimble, A. *The Salmon Rivers of England and Wales*, Kegan Paul 1913

Gray, L.N.R. *Torridge Fishery*, Nicholas Kaye 1957

Hals, William. Part I. *The complete History of Cornwall*, unpublished. Part II *The Parochial History of Cornwall*, part published, A. Brice 1750.

Hoskins, W.G. & Finberg, H. P. R. *Devonshire Studies*, Jonathan Cape 1952

Hoskins, W.G. *Devon*, Collins 1954

Hoskins, W.G. *Two Thousand Years in Exeter*, Phillimore, 1960

MacDermot, E.T. *The History of the Forest of Exmoor*, David & Charles Reprints 1973

Marshall, W. *The Rural Economy of the West of England*, David & Charles 1970

Moore, Rev. Thomas, *The History of Devonshire*, Robert Jennings 1829

Norway, A.H. *Highways and Byways in Devon and Cornwall*, Macmillan 1898

Notley, J.B.S. The River Avon 1880–1980 Private paper, Avon Fishing 1979

Polwhele, R. *The History of Cornwall*, Kohler & Coombes 1978

Pulman, George. *The Book of the Axe*, 1875

Stephan, Dom. John. *A History of Buckfast Abbey*, The Burleigh Press 1970

Webster, J. Salmon and Migratory Trout of the River Teign. A Lecture Delivered Before the Torquay Natural History Society 1889